Peaceful Patterns Coloring Therapy

Presents

"Joy in the Journey"

Coloring Therapy For All Ages

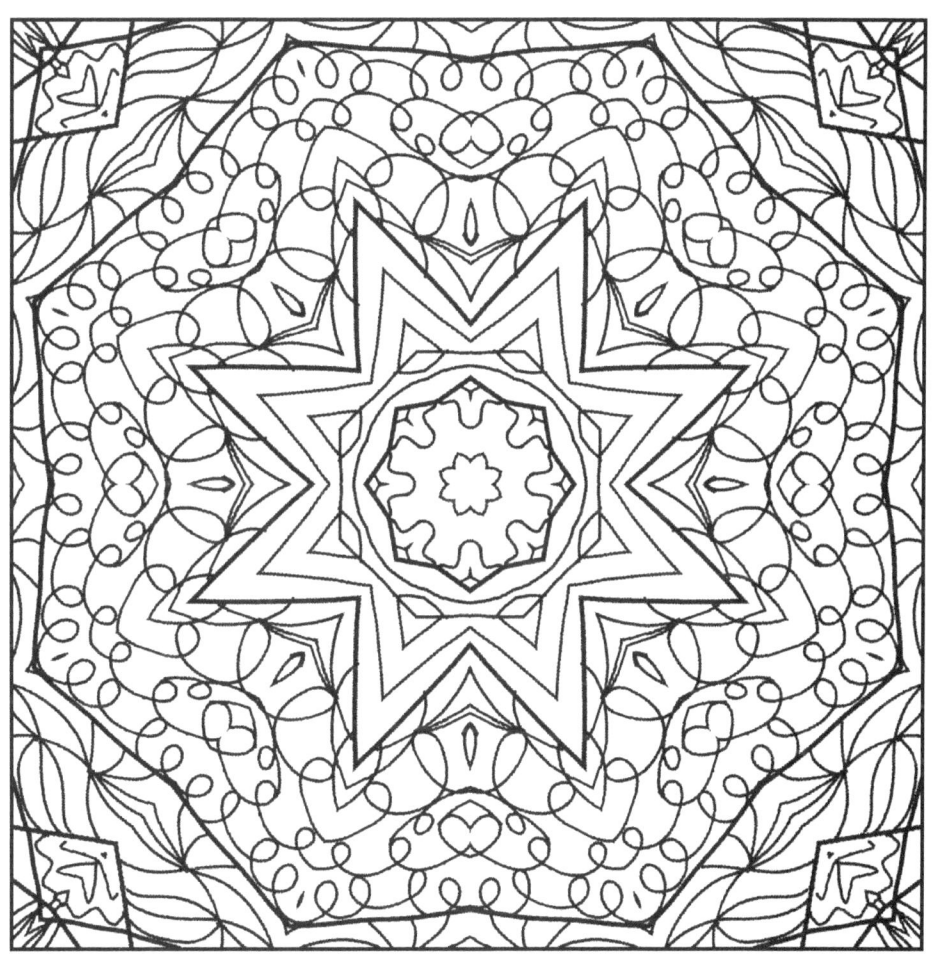

By: Bonnie K.T. Dillabough

DEDICATION

When I was very young, my grandmother, Juanita H. Tussey, spent hours with me and my sister teaching us to sketch, shade and color pictures of everything from the flowers in her lush garden to a tree or stream we encountered on our many camping trips. Art supplies such as crayons, colored pencils and sometime water colors were always made available to us to expand our creativity. Those were peaceful and happy memories. I hereby dedicate this book to "Mimi" with fondness and great gratitude for her loving care and the way she opened our eyes to this beautiful world.

Acknowledgements:

George C. Dillabough, Vera Martins Duncan, Bernadette Dimitrov, Jennifer Dillabough - Thank you so much for all of your support as colorists, artwork, editing advice and cheerleading.

Also a shout out to my TEAM Coloring Book authors and Bill Platt for introducing me to coloring book publishing.

It is with great joy that I present to you my first in a series of coloring books for people of all ages. This book has no pictures and there are no rules. "Peaceful Patterns – Joy in the Journey" is intended to allow the calming influence of creativity to heal and bless you. Take your time. Put on some joyful music. Choose the colors that attract you.

On each page is a "Happy Thought" to give you a spark and increase the joy in your life. Thinking of these "Happy Thoughts" while you color creates a mindful coloring experience. They come from some surprising sources, but all are for your uplift and joy as you are coloring.

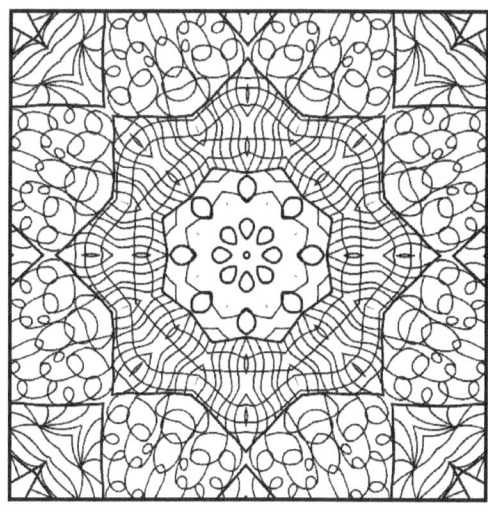

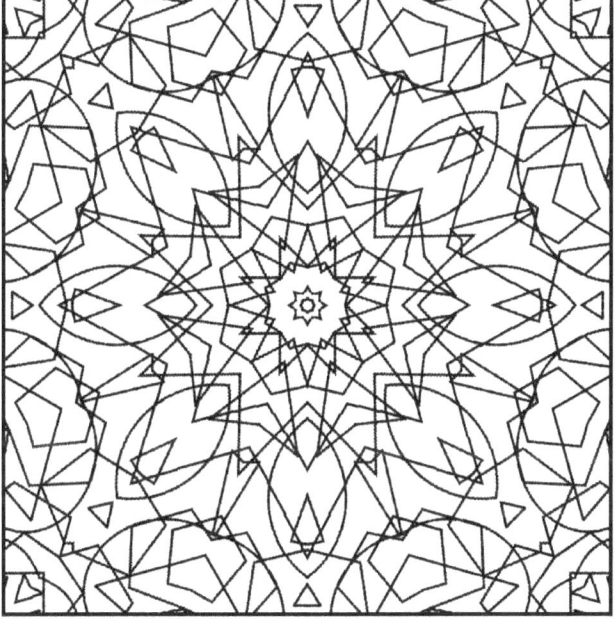

Recent studies have shown that the process of coloring has many benefits.

- Slows breathing and heart rate
- Lowers blood pressure
- Improves concentration
- Lowers stress levels
- Lifts the mind and emotions
- Stimulates creativity
- Not to mention all of the benefits of lower stress levels

Which is why more and more adults are coloring for their health as well as the sheer enjoyment of the creative process. In addition, coloring is often part of the therapy for depression, PTSD and other mental and emotional issues.

(Please note: Coloring is not a substitute for getting professional help for your health problems, physical, emotional or mental.)

As a bonus for all of you who bought or were given this book, you are invited to a special, private group on Facebook specifically for you.

In the group, you can show off your latest finished pages, chat with other colorists and be the first to hear of new coloring books on the market. (Not just mine). In addition, I will be introducing mp3s of amazing, relaxing music to go along with your coloring

When you share pages you have colored, there will be prizes, including gift cards to allow you to buy mp3s or coloring pencils or more coloring books. All because I appreciate you and want you to have an amazing overall experience.

ATTENTION:

To get your free pass into the Facebook group, simply register your book at:

PeacefulPatternsColoringTherapy.com/VIP

You will be asked for your name and email address. I personally guarantee that none of your information will ever be sold or distributed to anyone.

We value our VIP members and promise only amazing information and news related to coloring.

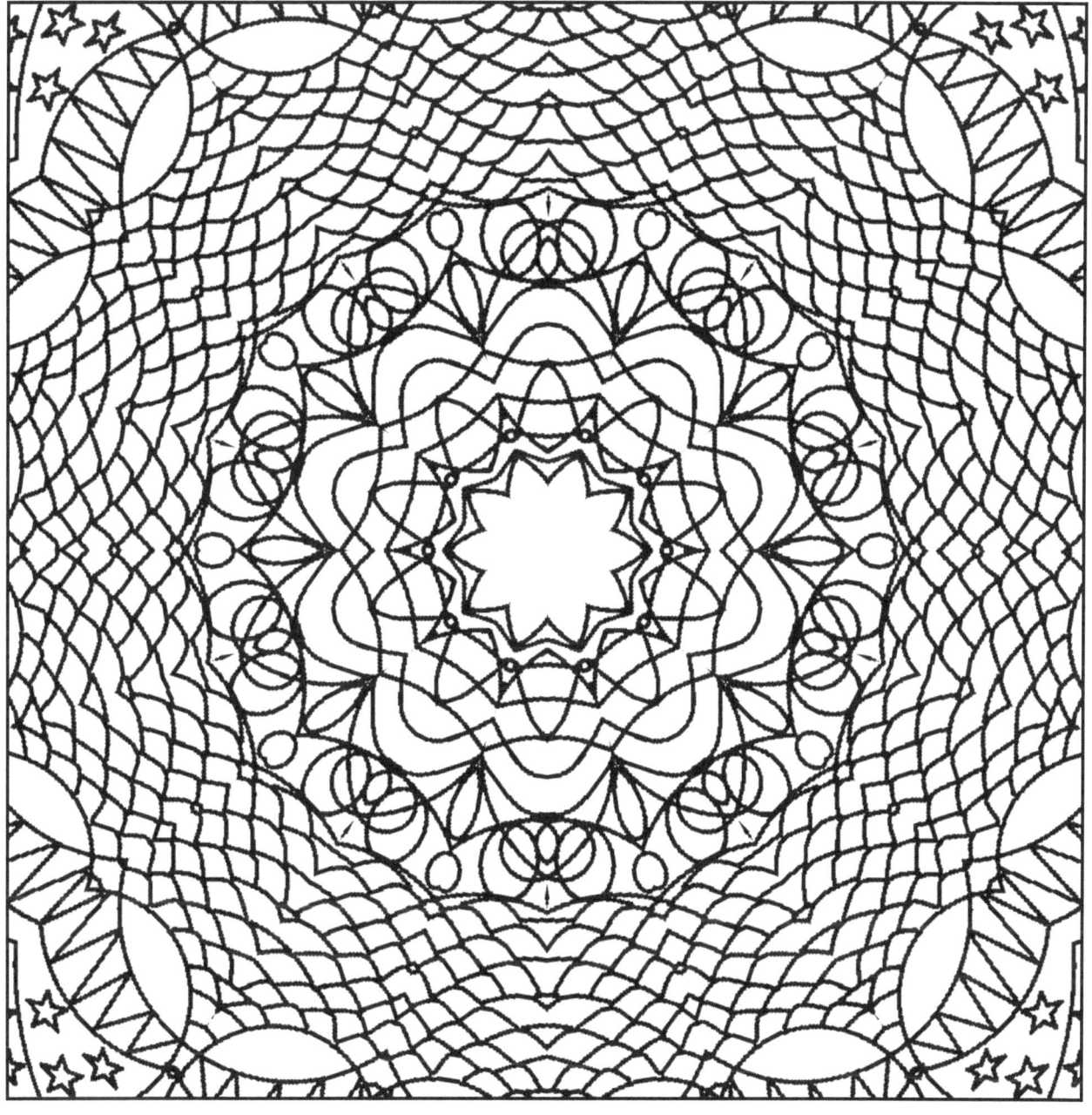

Happy Thought:

"Today I choose life. Every morning when I wake up I can choose joy, happiness, negativity, pain... To feel the freedom that comes from being able to continue to make mistakes and choices - today I choose to feel life, not to deny my humanity but embrace it."

~~Kevyn Aucoin~~

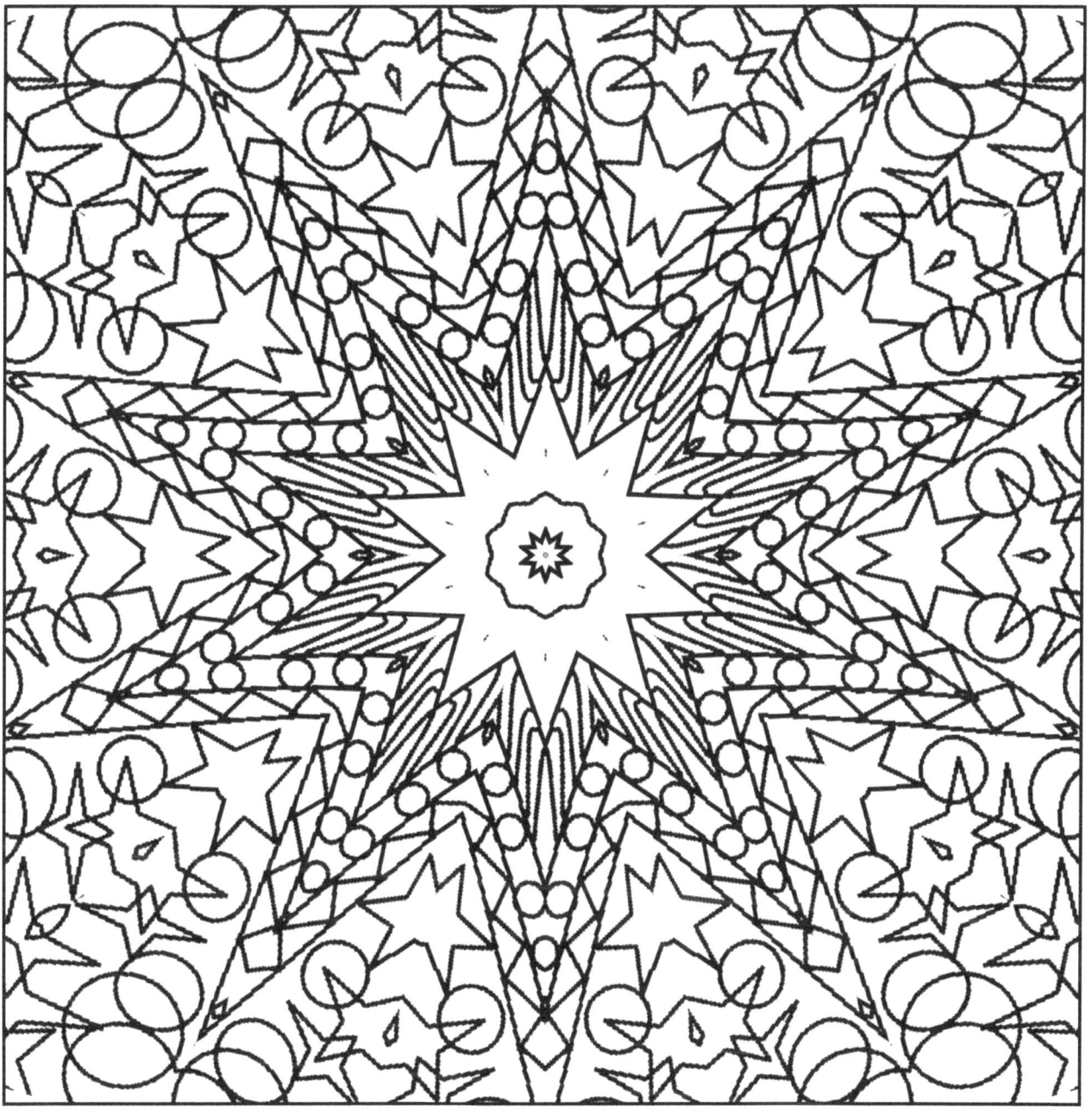

Happy Thought:

"The joy of life comes from our encounters with new experiences, and hence there is no greater joy than to have an endlessly changing horizon, for each day to have a new and different sun."

~~Christopher McCandless~~

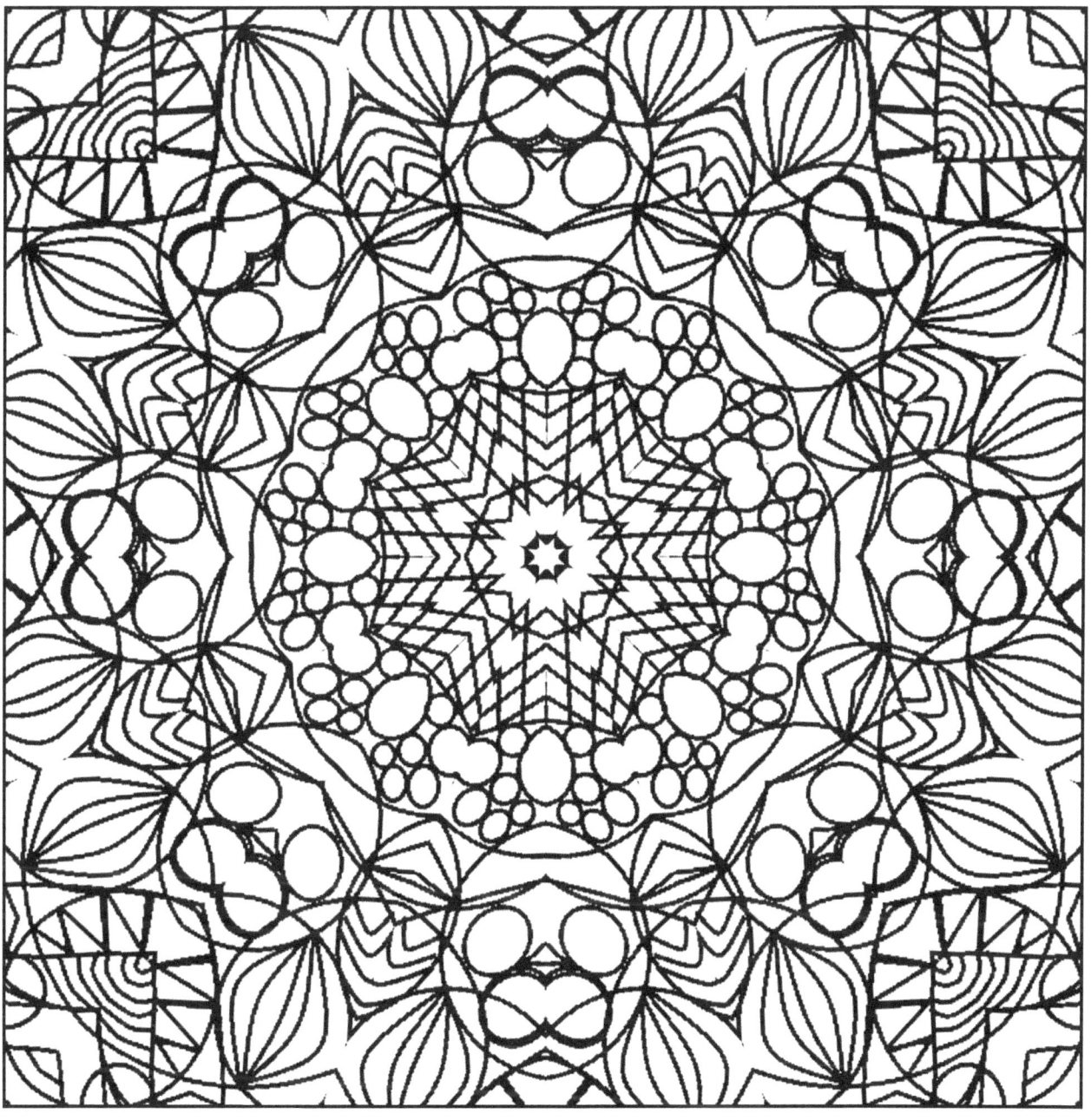

Happy Thought:

"If we're destroying our trees and destroying our environment and hurting animals and hurting one another and all that stuff, there's got to be a very powerful energy to fight that. I think we need more love in the world. We need more kindness, more compassion, more joy, more laughter. I definitely want to contribute to that."

~~Ellen DeGeneres~~

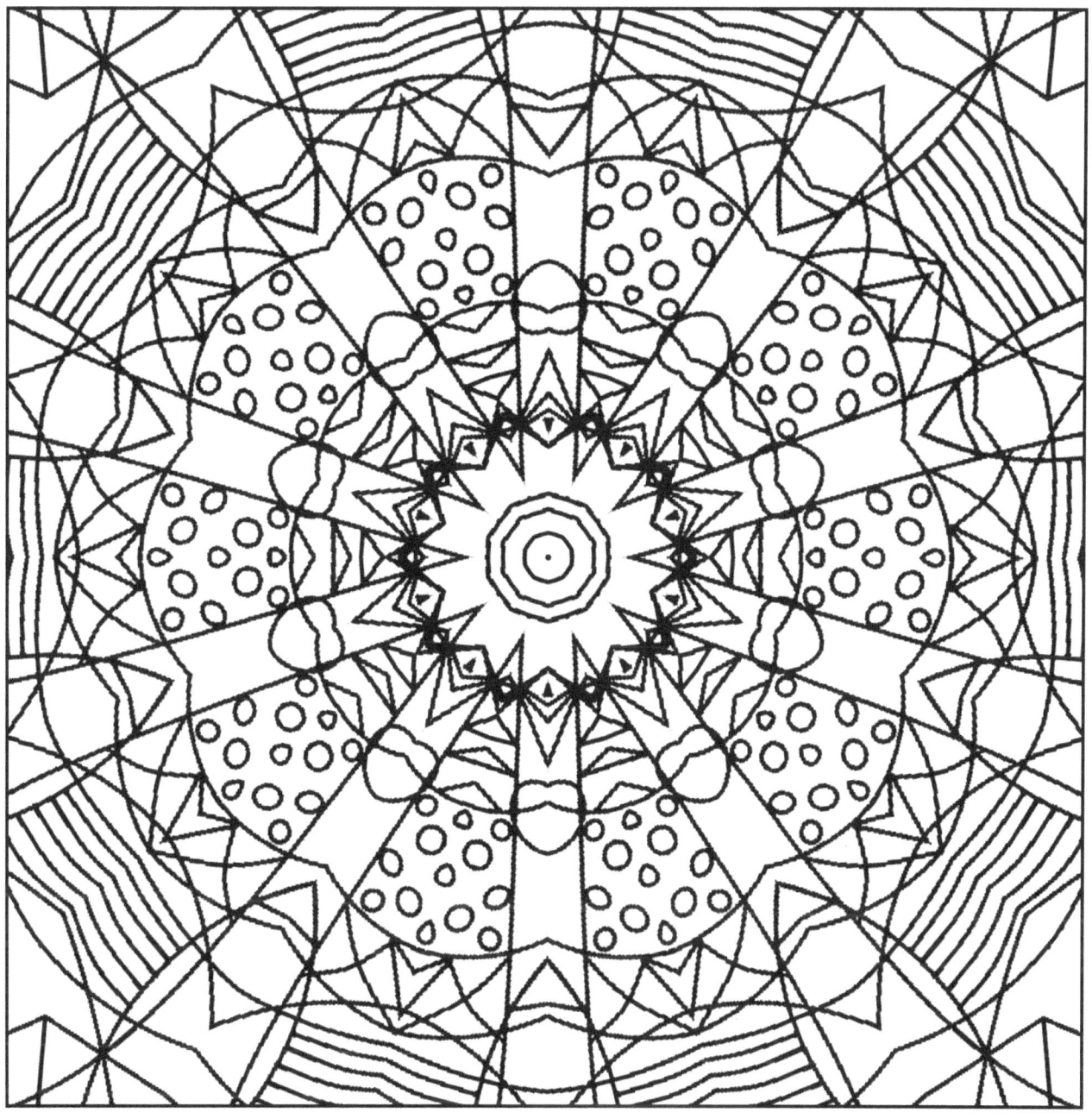

Happy Thought:

"Gratitude can transform common days into thanksgivings, turn routine jobs into joy, and change ordinary opportunities into blessings."

~~William Arthur Ward~~

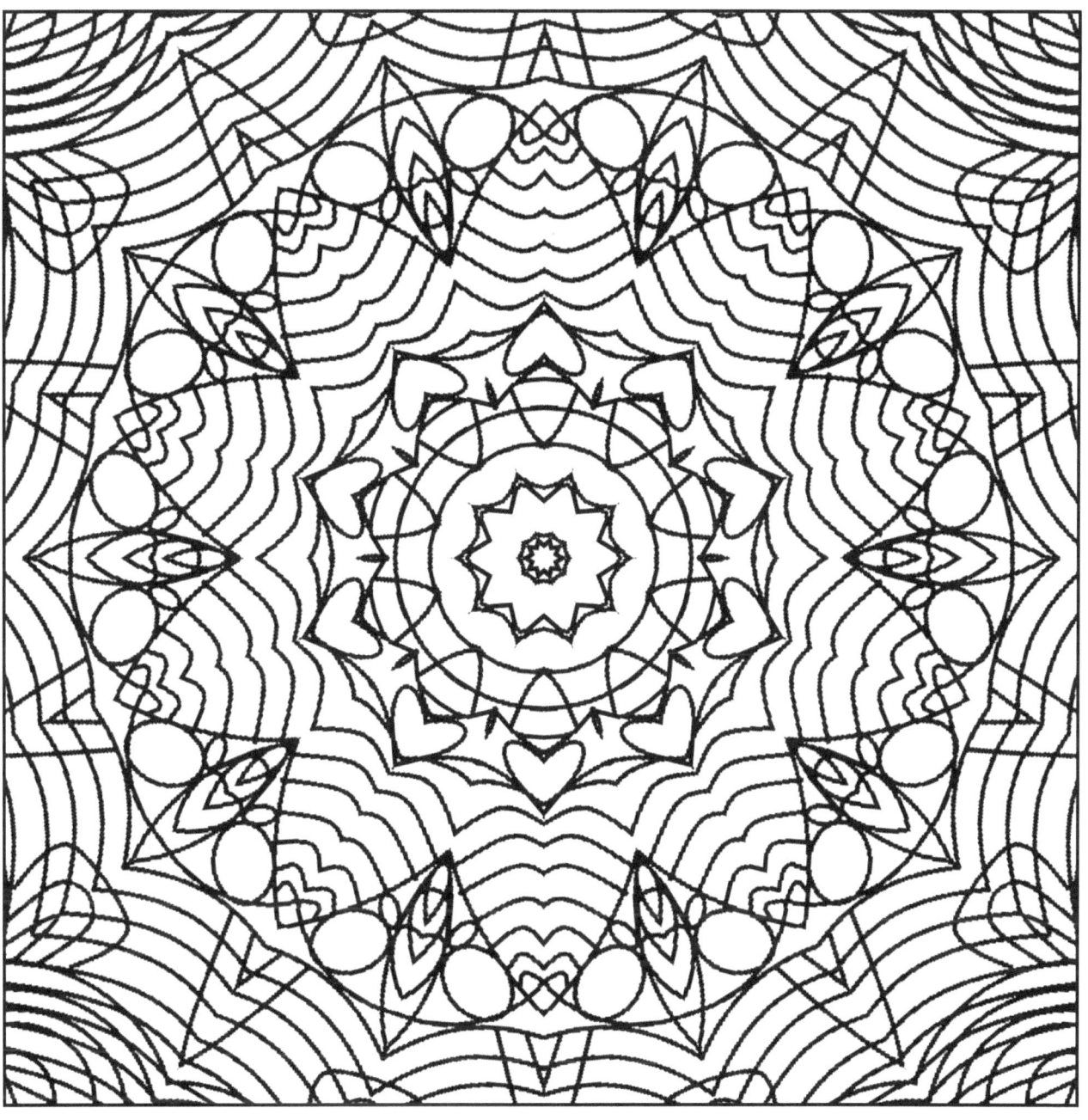

Happy Thought:

"The single overriding objective in wellness is creating constant personal renewal where we recognize and act on the truth that each day is a miraculous gift, and our job is to untie the ribbons. That's the Law of Esprit: living life with joy."

~~Greg Anderson~~

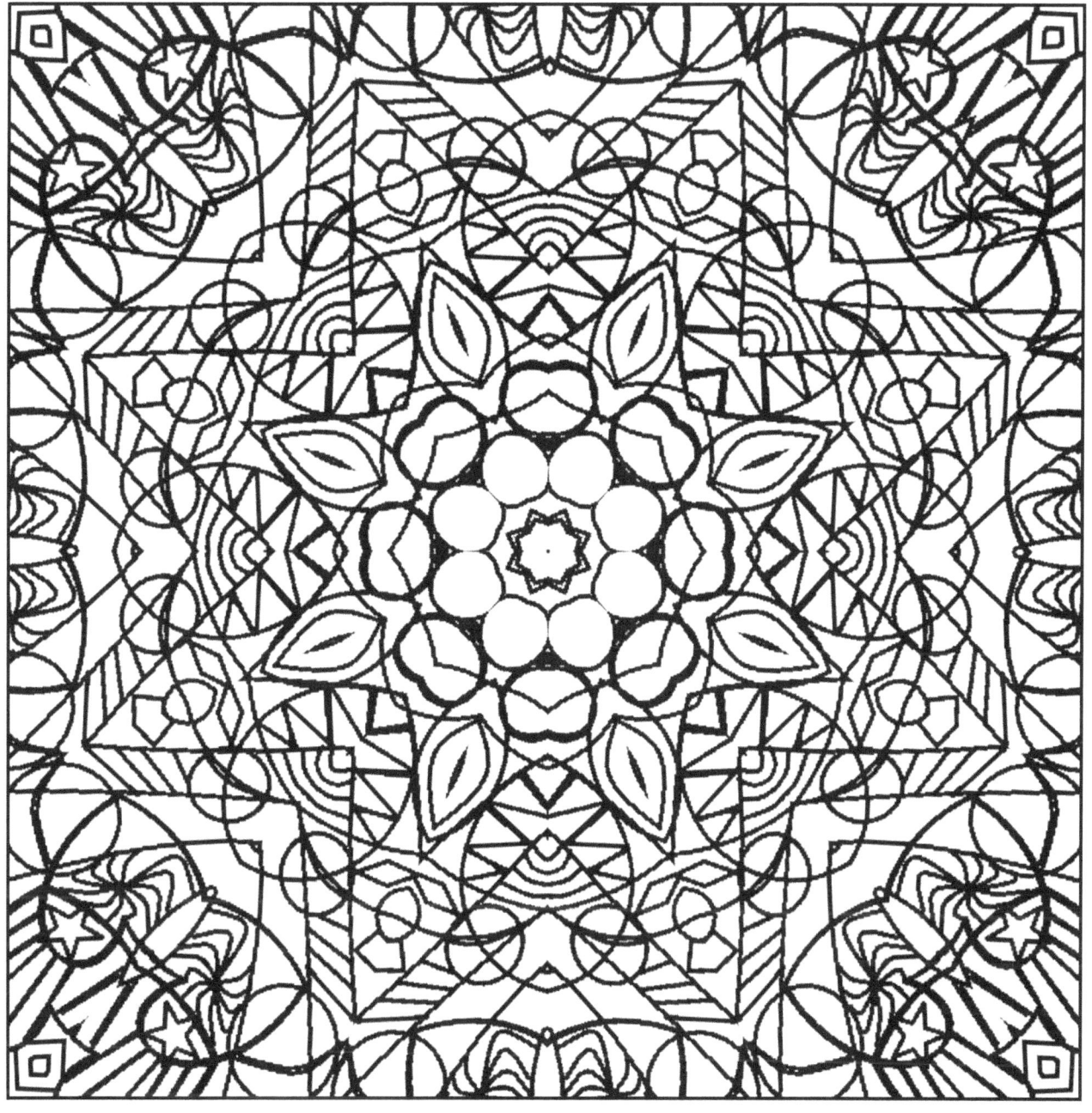

Happy Thought:

"My dad would go to work every day and write in a room full of funny people. He enjoyed it. I know great writers who find the process agonizing but to me, writing has always been sheer joy."

~~Joss Whedon~~

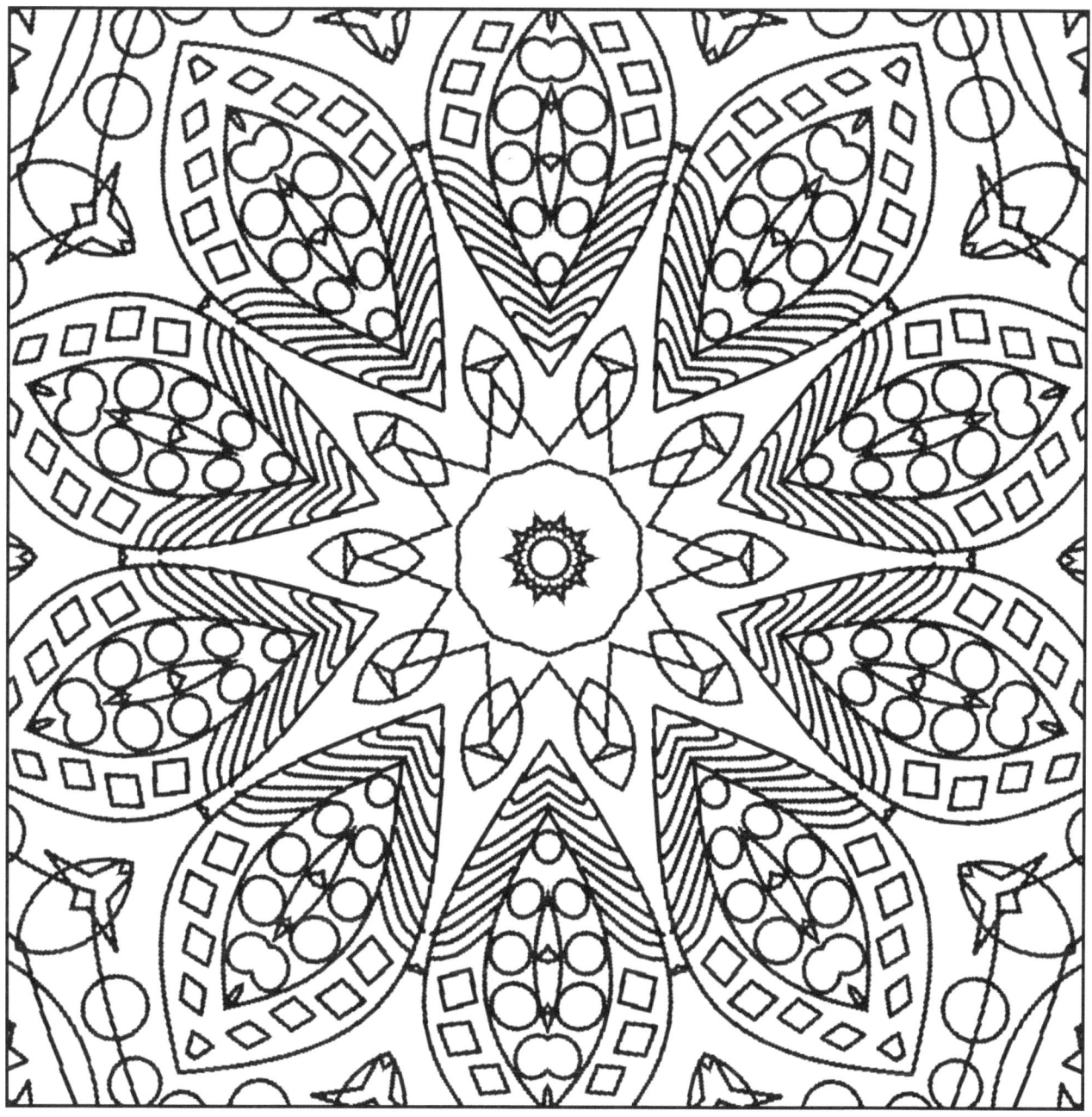

Happy Thought:

"Remarkable contributions are typically spawned by a passionate commitment to transcendent values such as beauty, truth, wisdom, justice, charity, fidelity, joy, courage and honor."

~~Gary Hamel~~

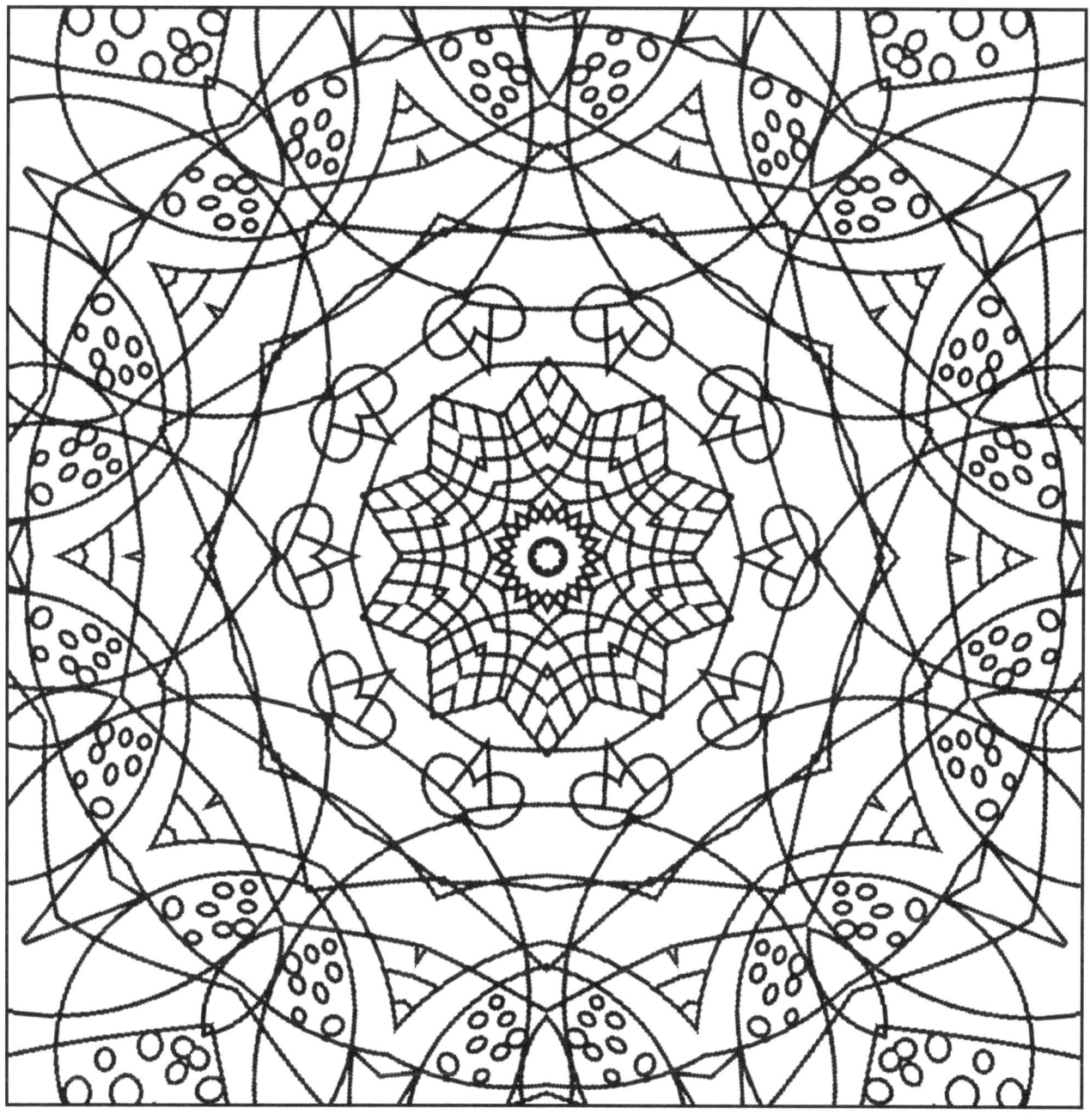

Happy Thought:

"The marvelous richness of human experience would lose something of rewarding joy if there were no limitations to overcome. The hilltop hour would not be half so wonderful if there were no dark valleys to traverse."

~~Helen Keller~~

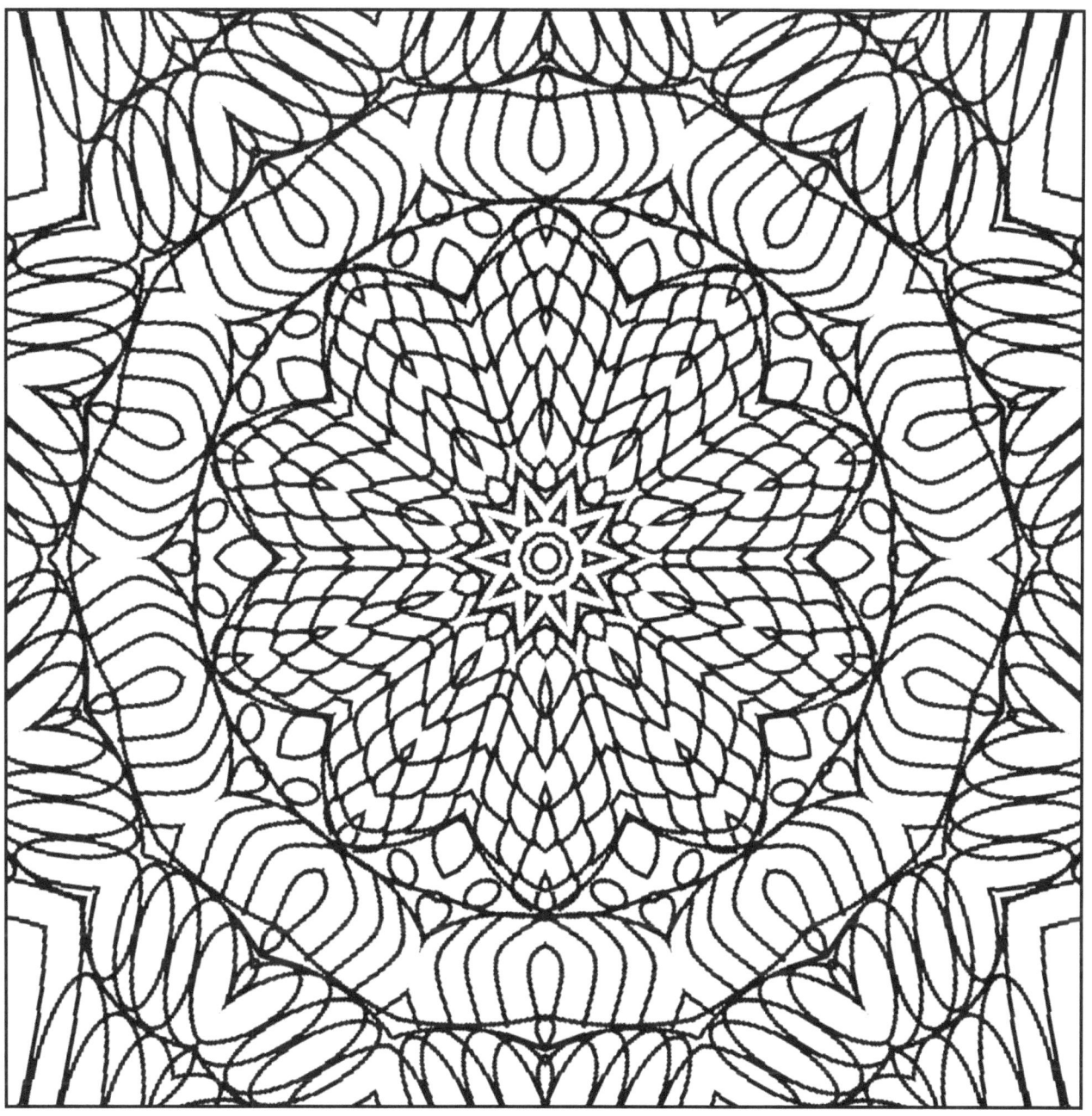

Happy Thought:

"People from a planet without flowers would think we must be mad with joy the whole time to have such things about us."

~~Iris Murdoch~~

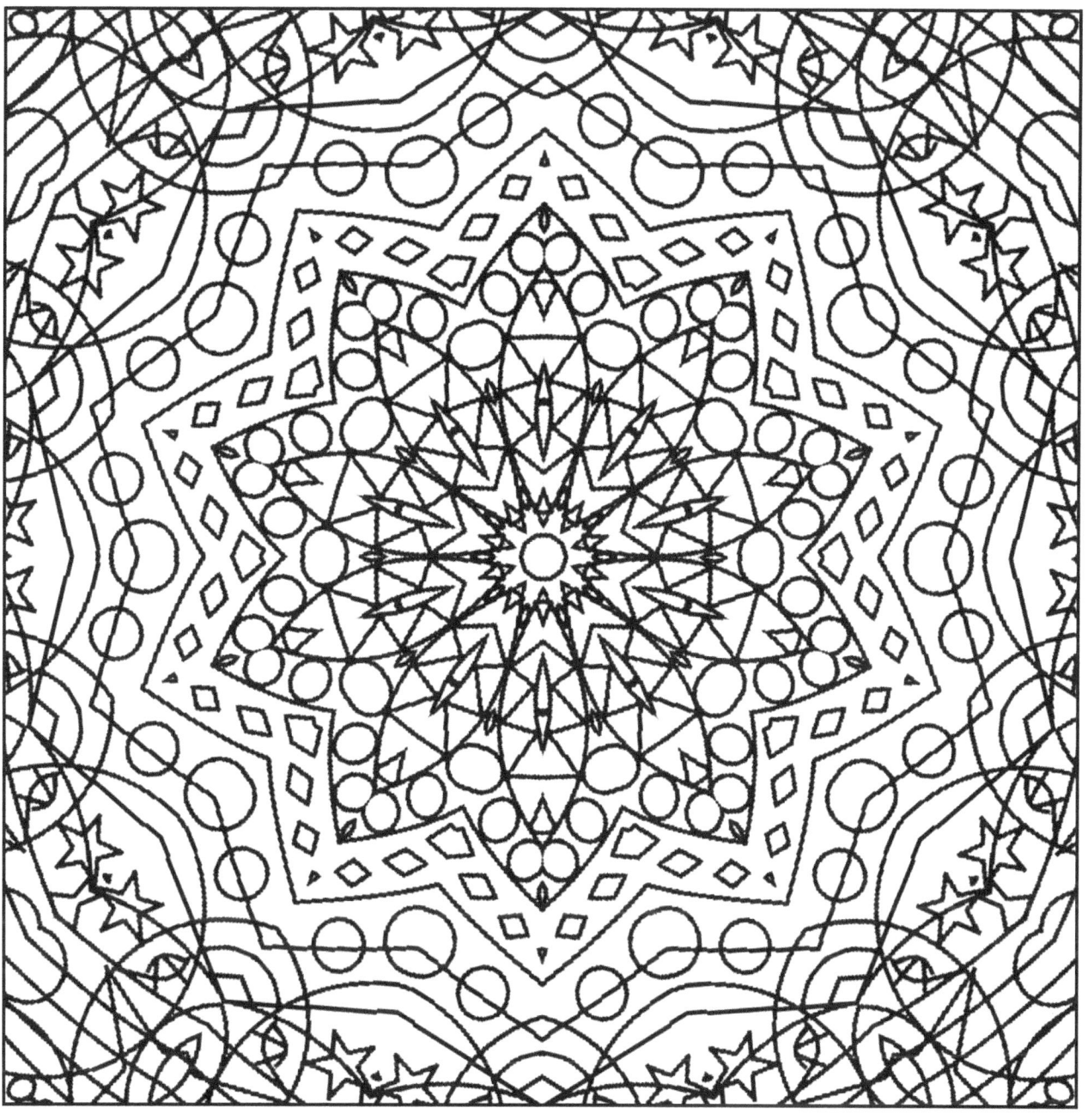

Happy Thought:

"Every person - with his or her own skills, abilities and uniqueness - can contribute to others and bring great joy to those that fortune has not smiled upon."

~~Shari Arison~~

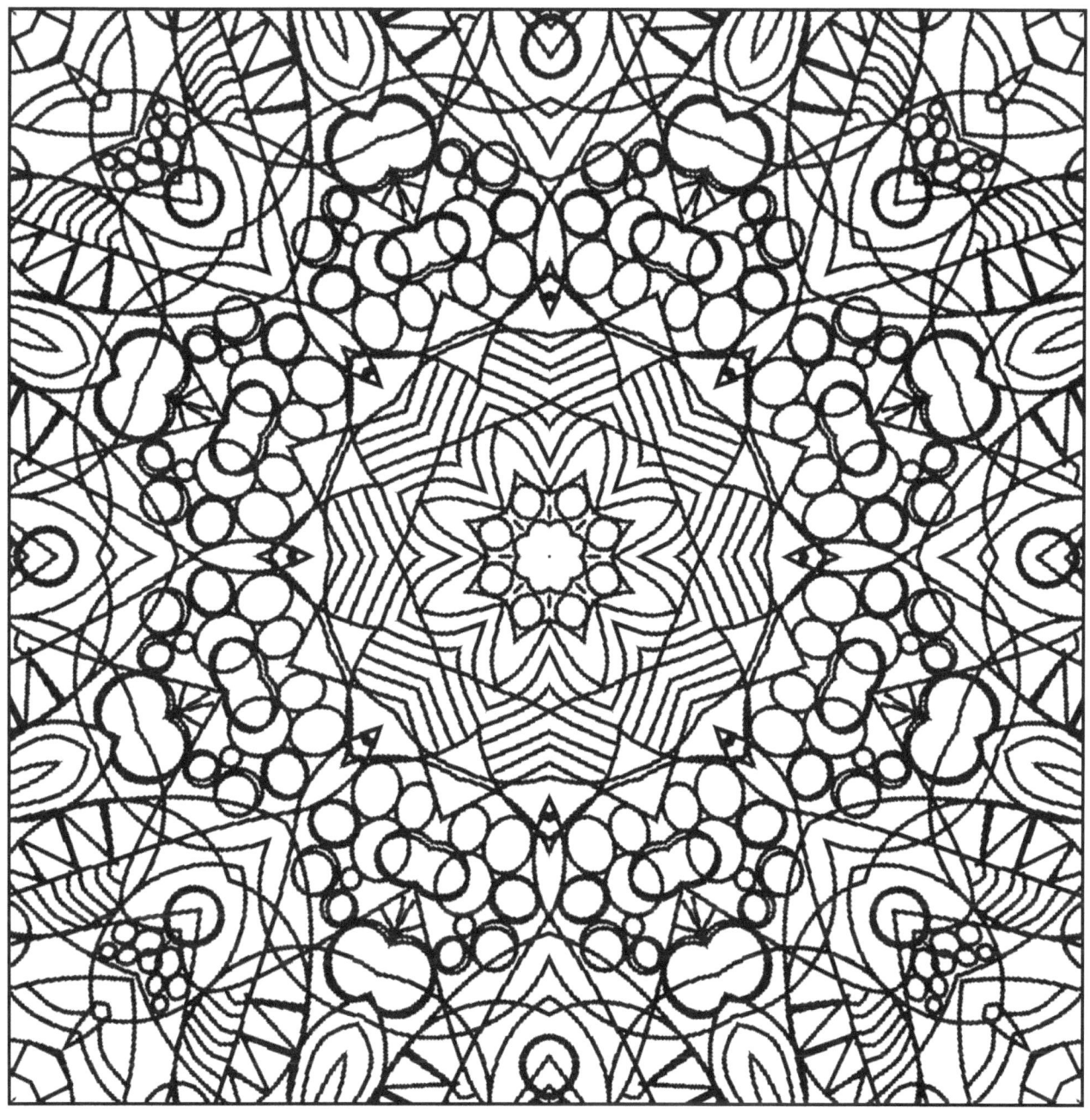

Happy Thought:

"The sharing of joy, whether physical, emotional, psychic, or intellectual, forms a bridge between the sharers which can be the basis for understanding much of what is not shared between them, and lessens the threat of their difference."

~~Audre Lorde~~

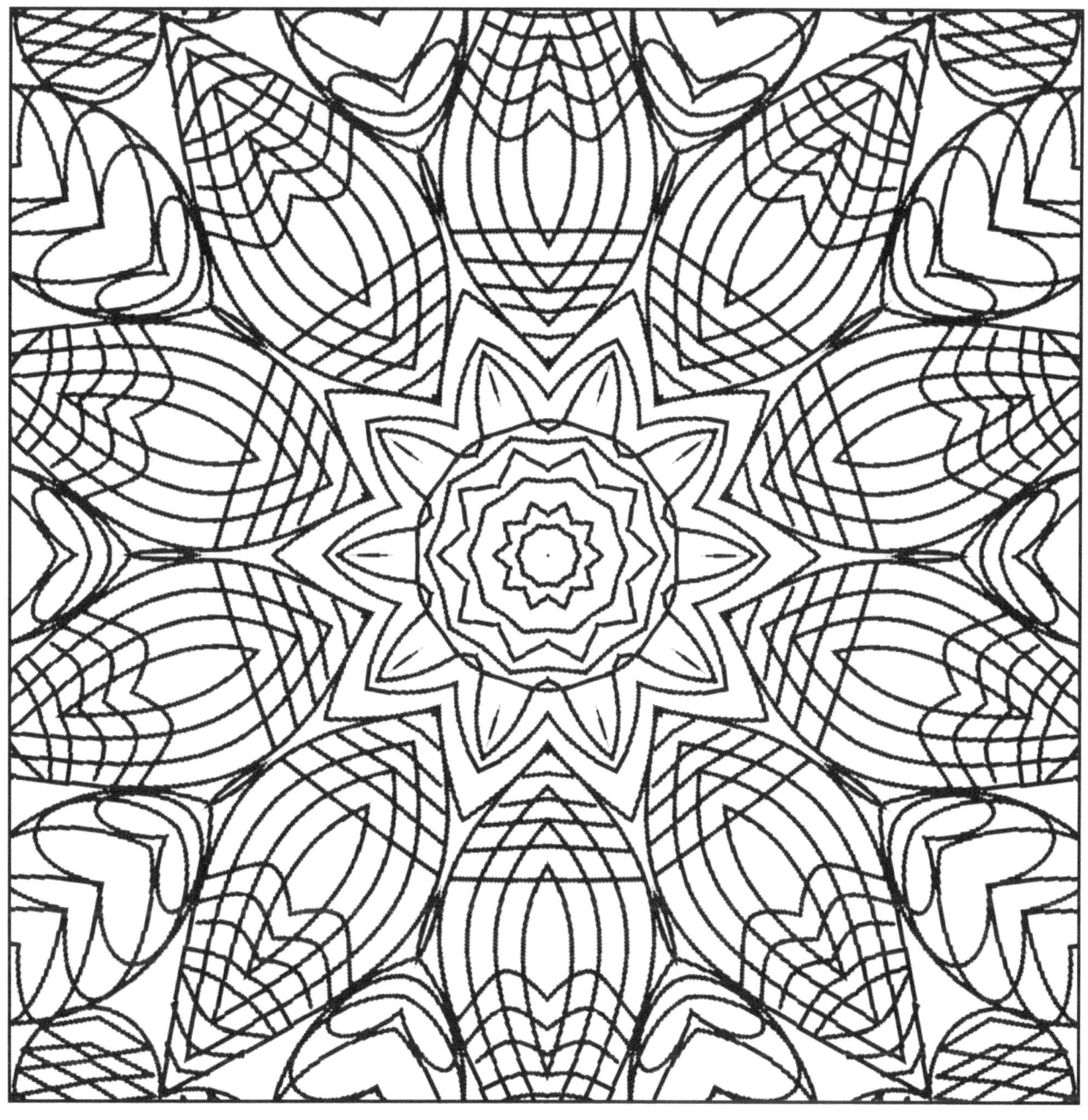

Happy Thought:

"To make others less happy is a crime. To make ourselves unhappy is where all crime starts. We must try to contribute joy to the world. That is true no matter what our problems, our health, our circumstances. We must try. I didn't always know this, and am happy I lived long enough to find it out."

~~Roger Ebert~~

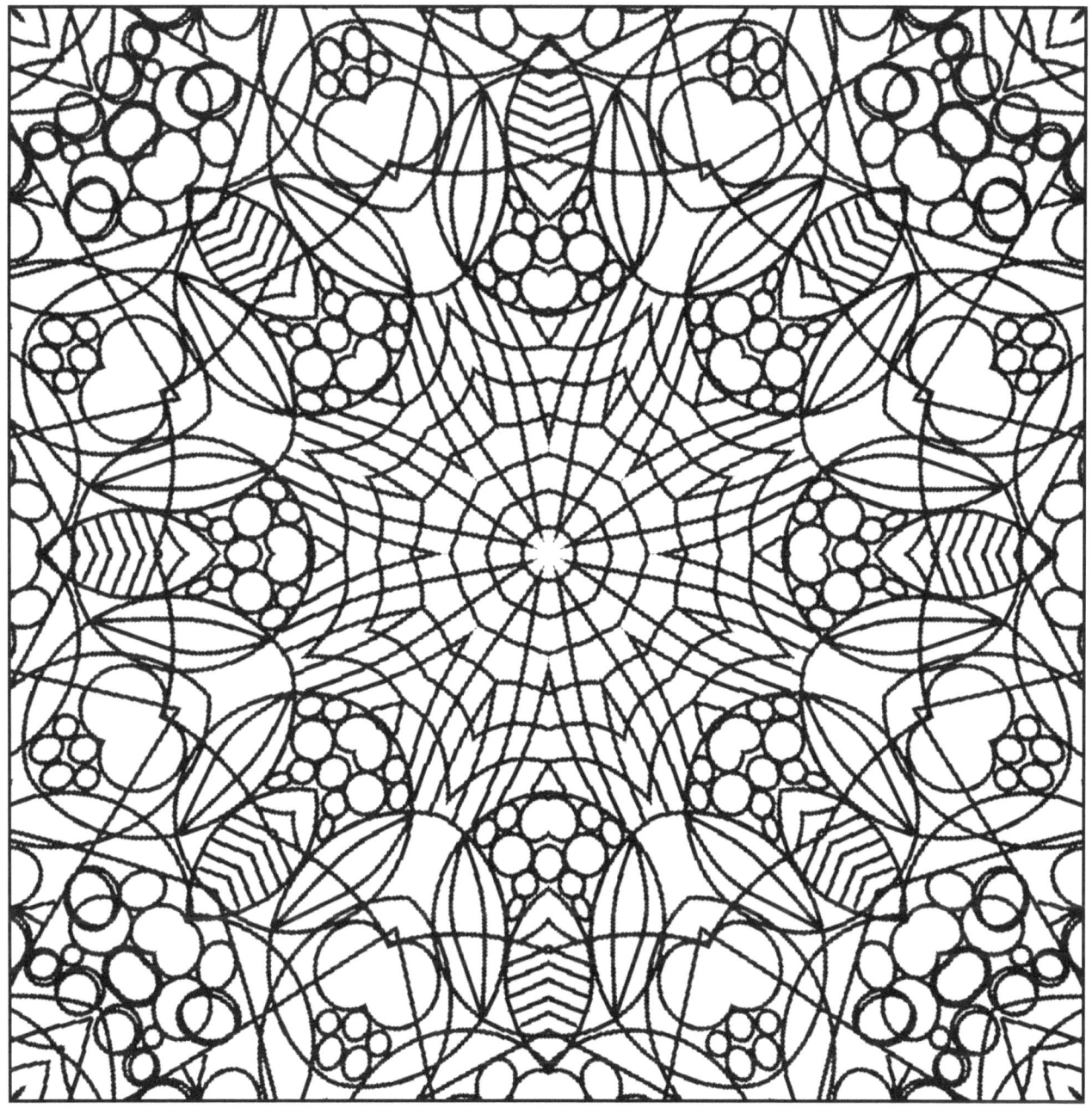

Happy Thought:

"When you're in the day-to-day grind, it just seems like it's another step along the way. But I find joy in the actual process, the journey, the work. It's not the end. It's not the end event."

-Cal Ripken, Jr.~~

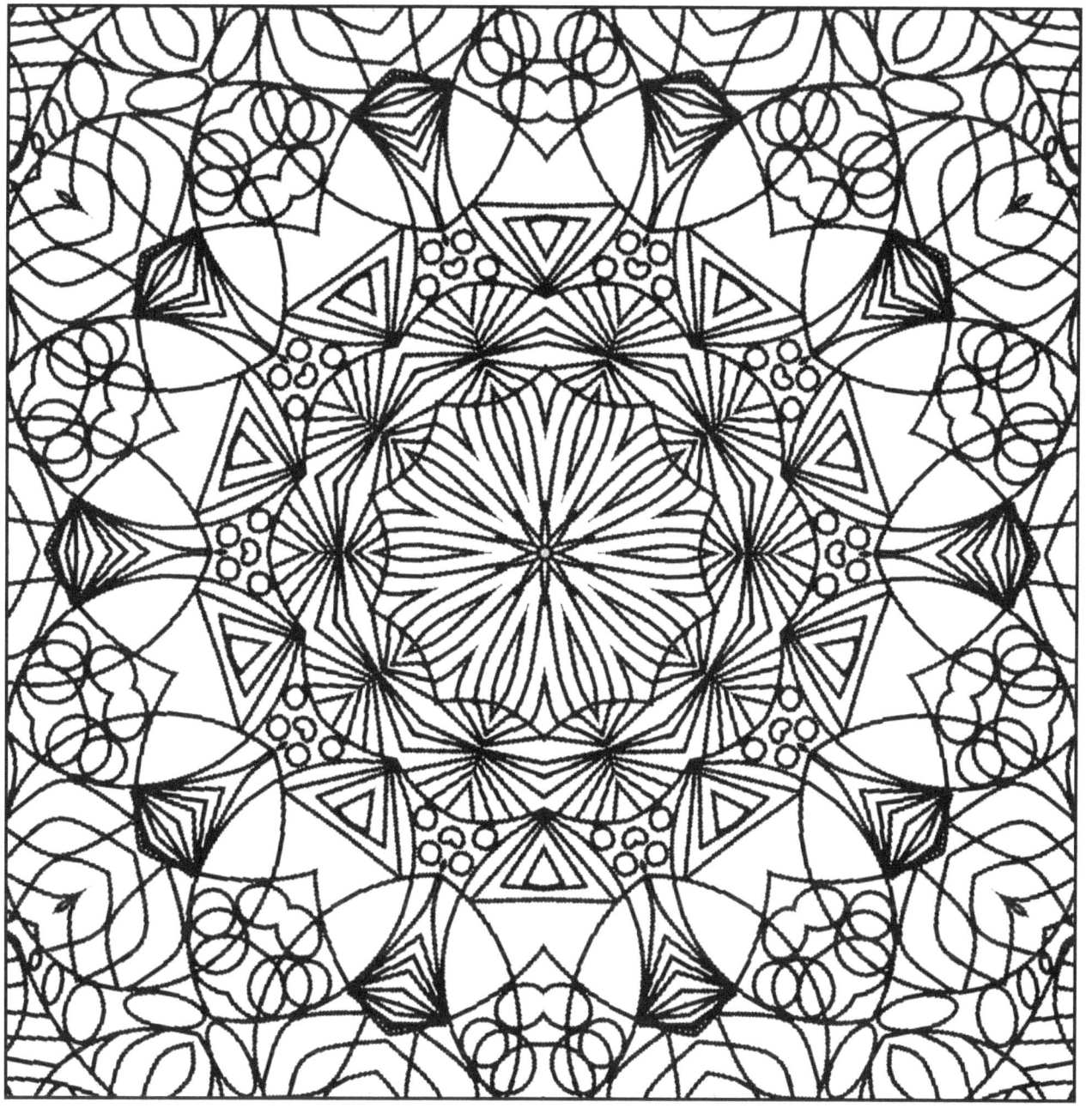

Happy Thought:

"If the sight of the blue skies fills you with joy, if a blade of grass springing up in the fields has power to move you, if the simple things of nature have a message that you understand, rejoice, for your soul is alive."

~~Eleonora Duse~~

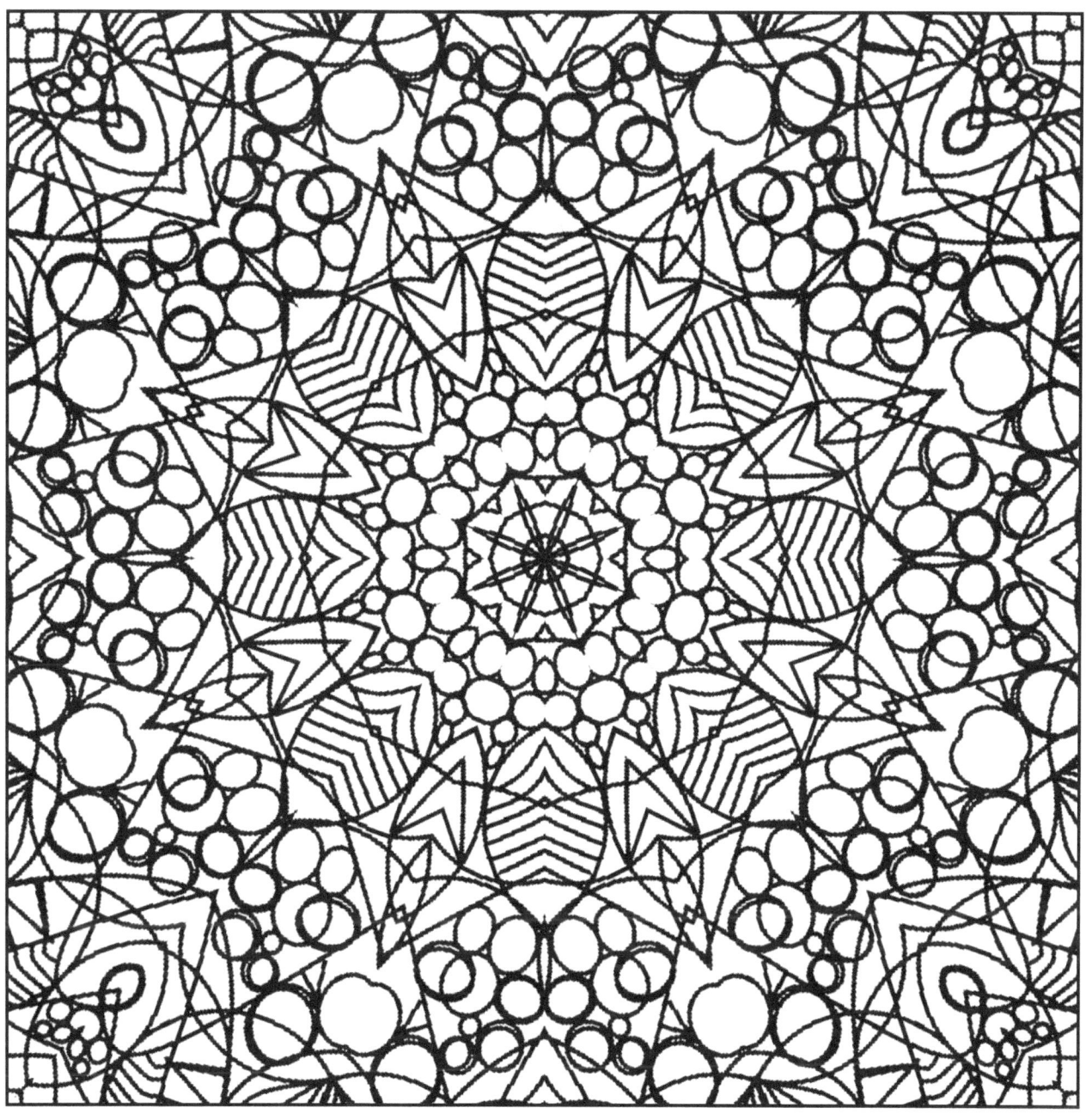

Happy Thought:

"There is no glory in star or blossom till looked upon by a loving eye;
There is no fragrance in April breezes till breathed with joy as they
wander by."

~~William C. Bryant~~

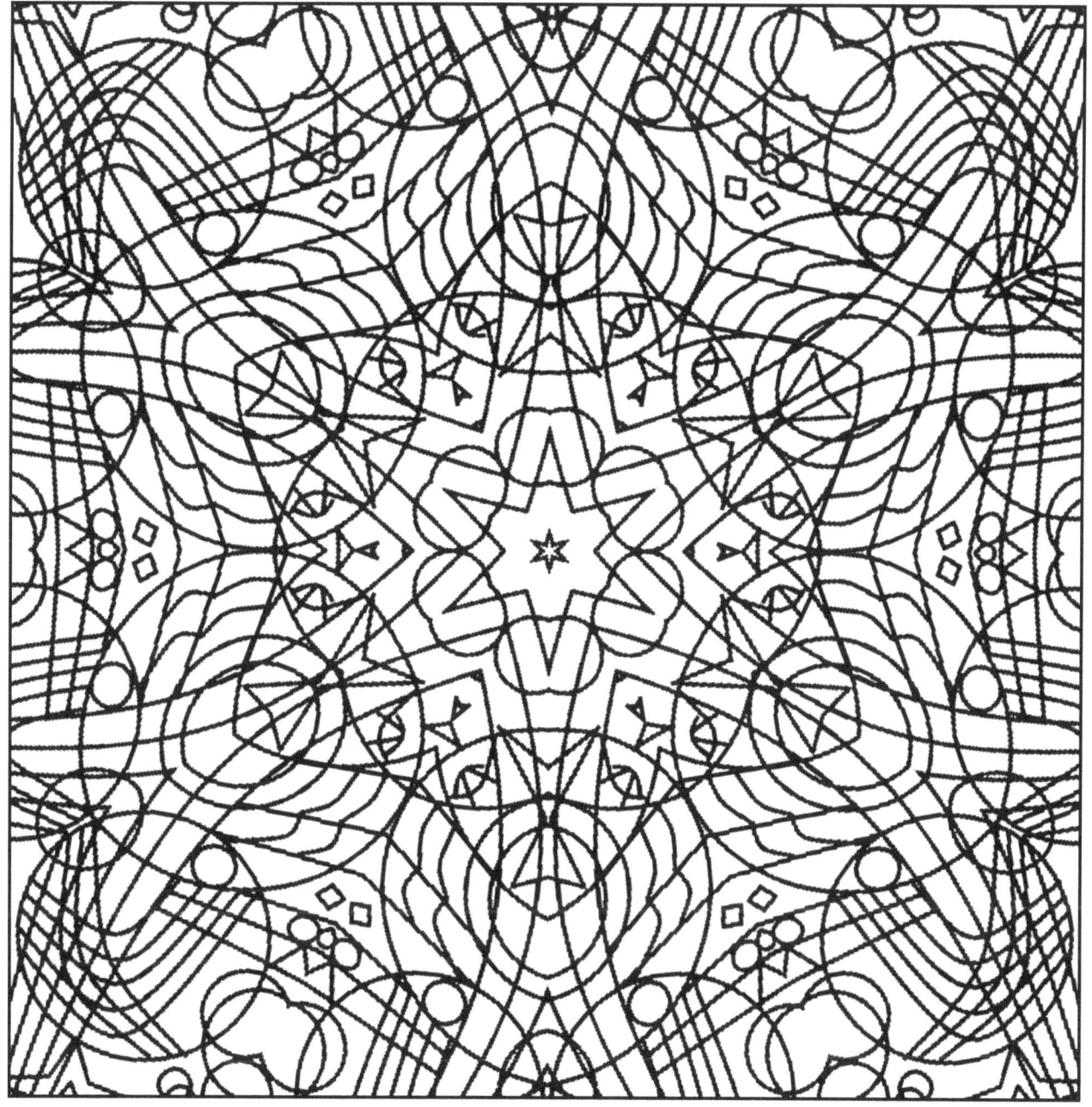

Happy Thought:

"Whoever renders service to many puts himself in line for greatness - great wealth, great return, great satisfaction, great reputation, and great joy."

~~Jim Rohn~~

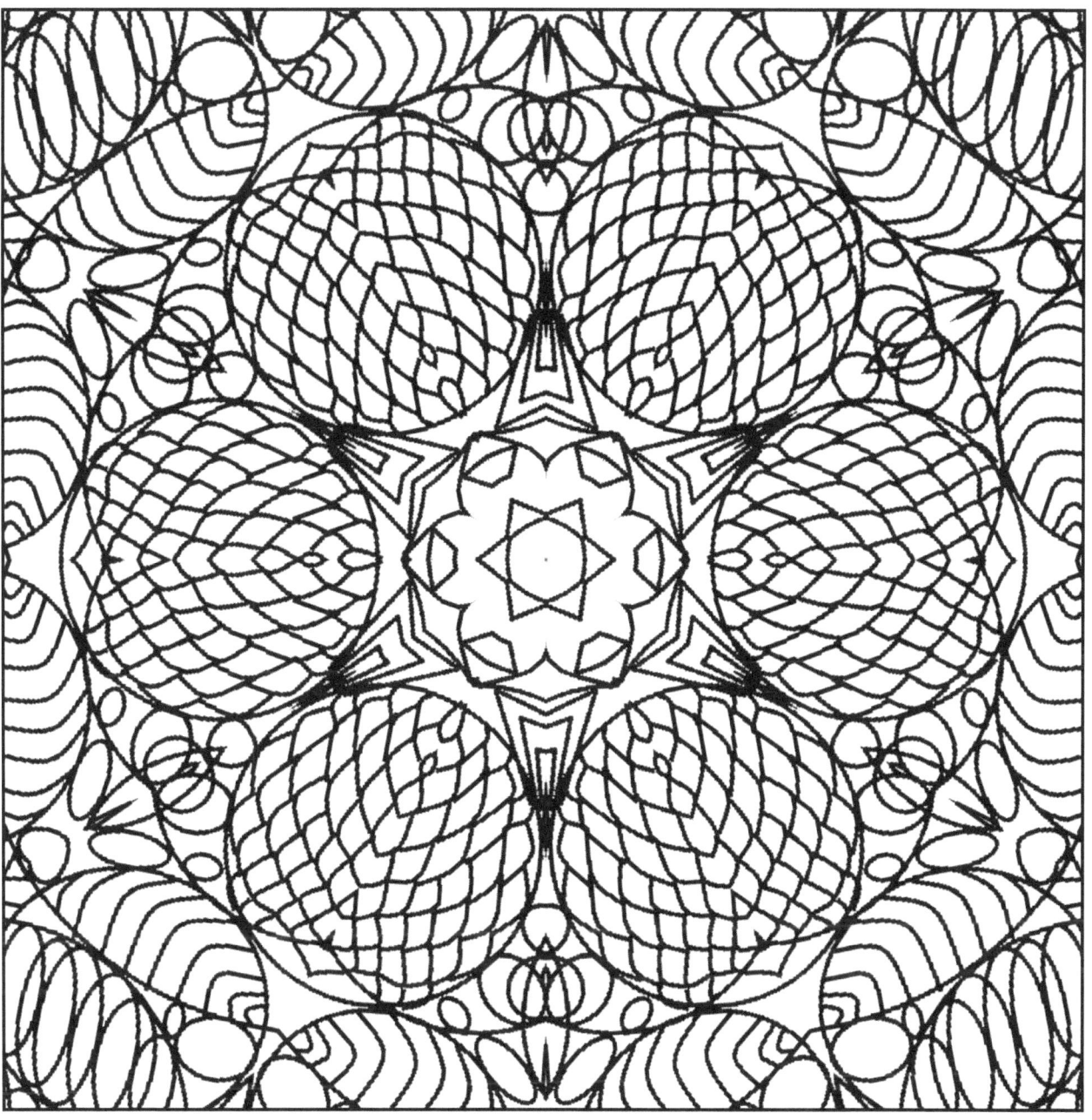

Happy Thought:

"Participate joyfully in the sorrows of the world. We cannot cure the world of sorrows, but we can choose to live in joy."

~~Joseph Campbell~~

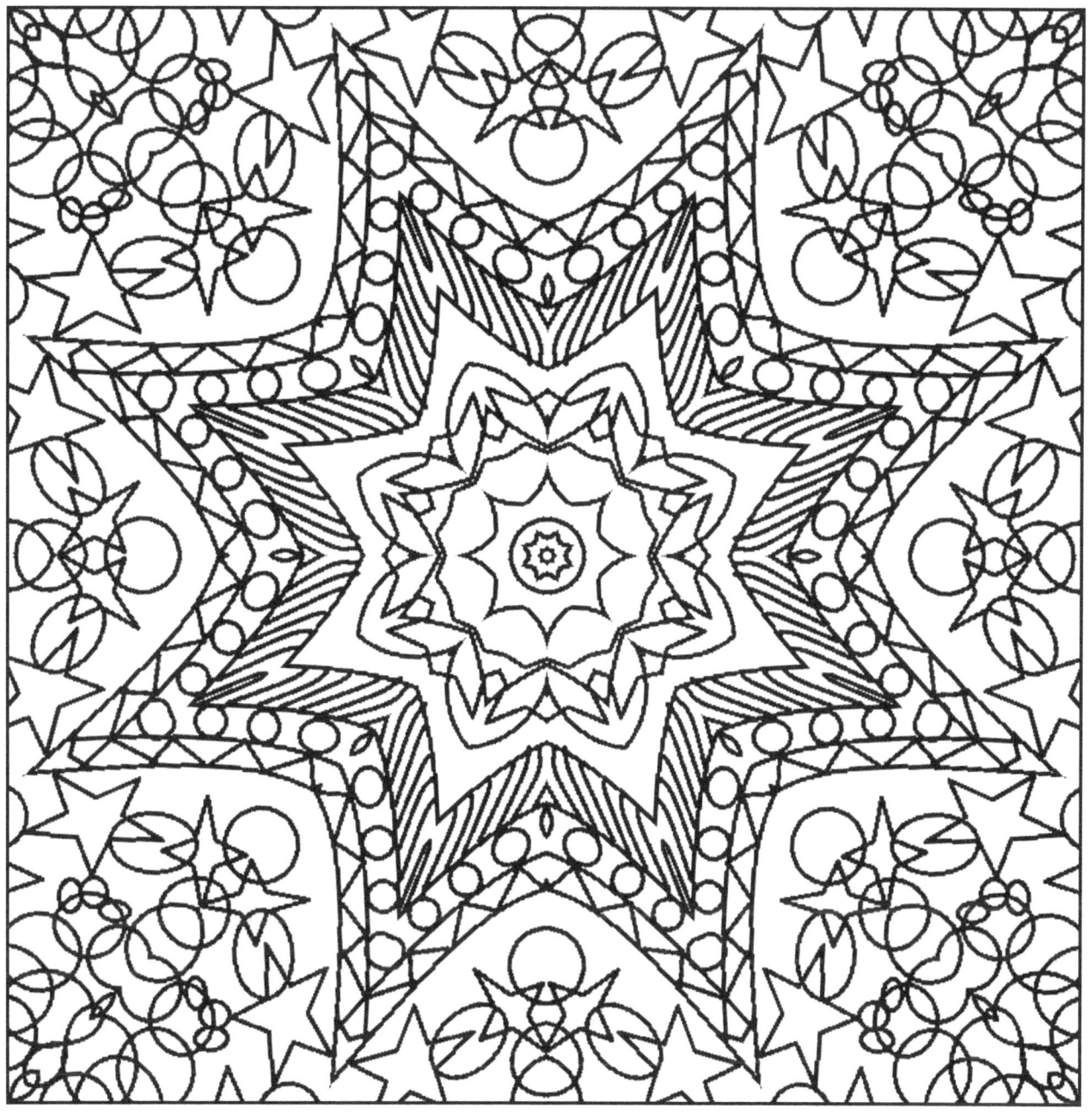

Happy Thought:

"Joy, rather than happiness, is the goal of life, for joy is the emotion which accompanies our fulfilling our natures as human beings. It is based on the experience of one's identity as a being of worth and dignity."

~~Rollo May~~

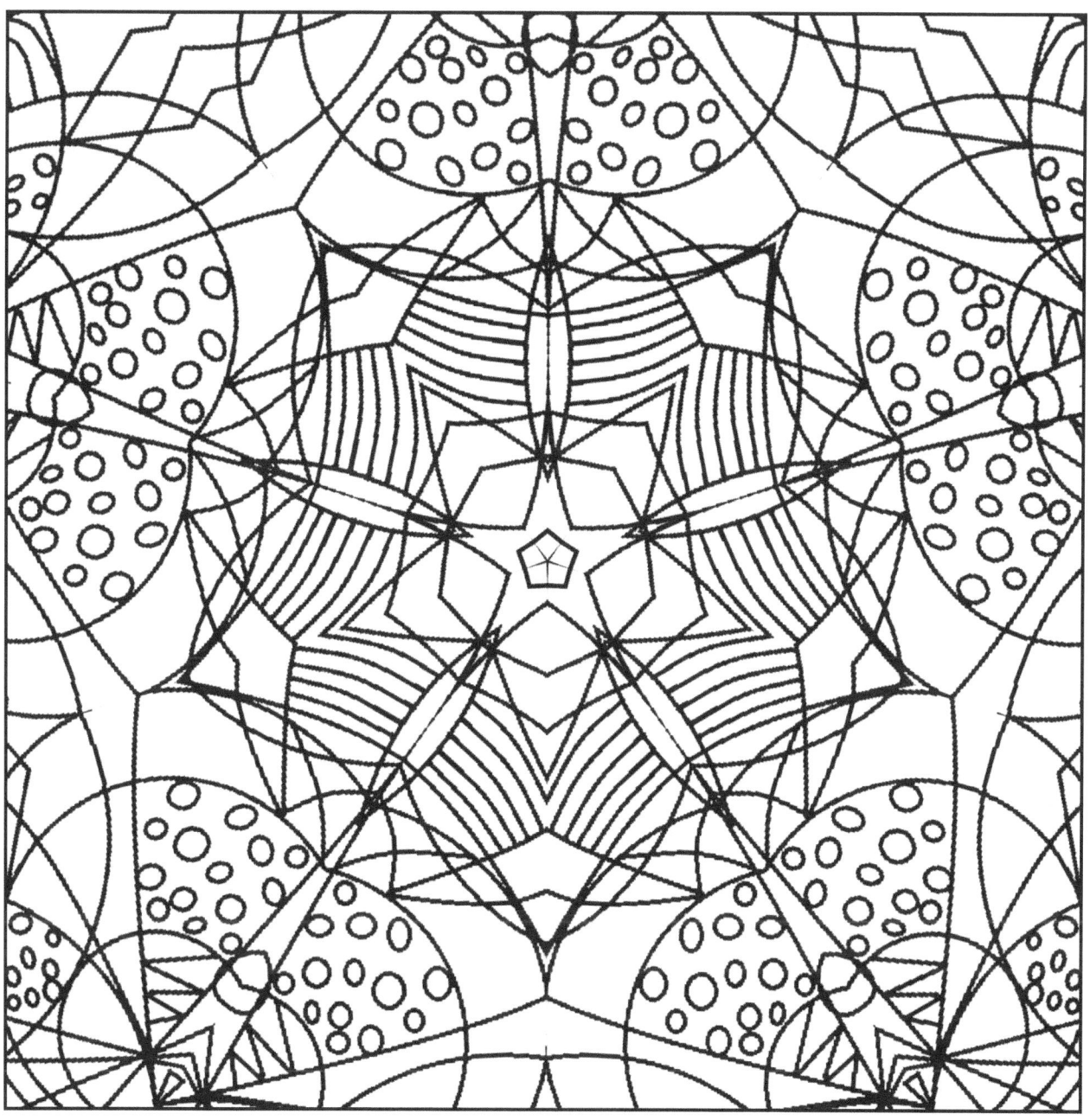

Happy Thought:

"There are seasons in life. Don't ever let anyone try to deny you the joy of one season because they believe you should stay in another season... Listen to yourself. Trust your instincts. Keep your perspective."

~~Jane Clayson~~

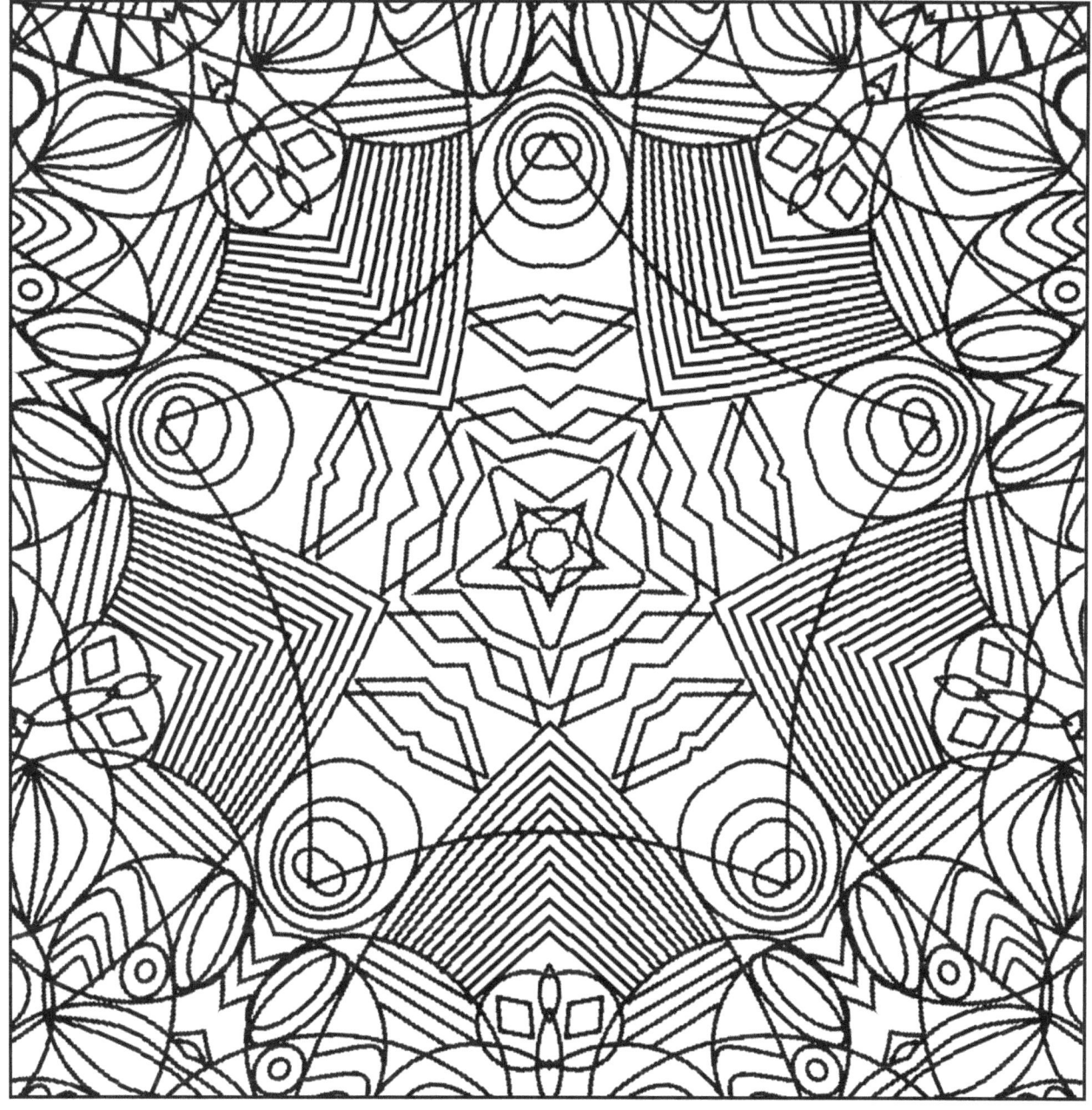

Happy Thought:

"My mother is a big believer in being responsible for your own happiness. She always talked about finding joy in small moments and insisted that we stop and take in the beauty of an ordinary day. When I stop the car to make my kids really see a sunset, I hear my mother's voice and smile."

~~Jennifer Garner~~

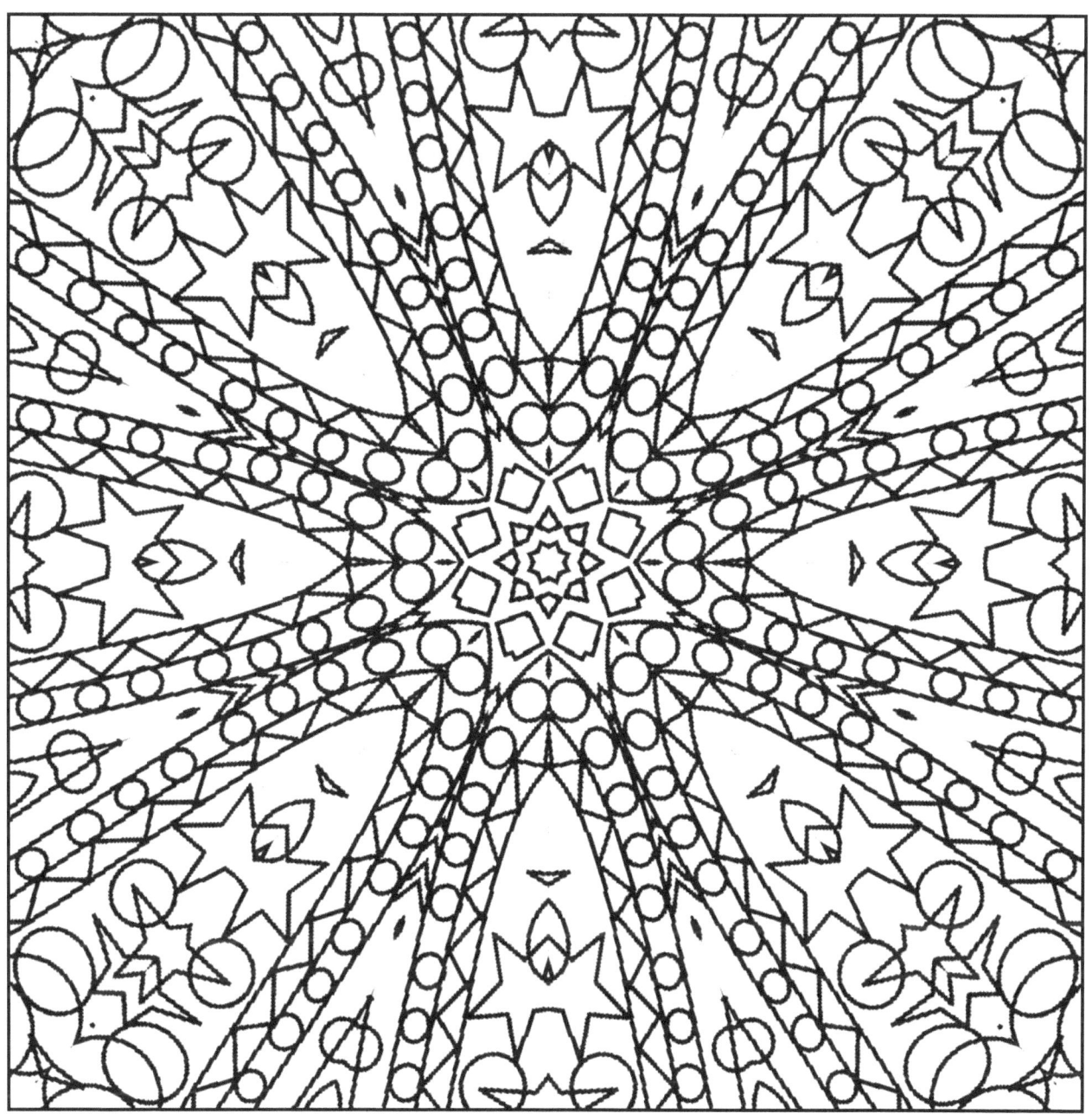

Happy Thought:

"Use those talents you have. You will make it. You will give joy to the world. Take this tip from nature: The woods would be a very silent place if no birds sang except those who sang best."

~~Bernard Meltzer~~

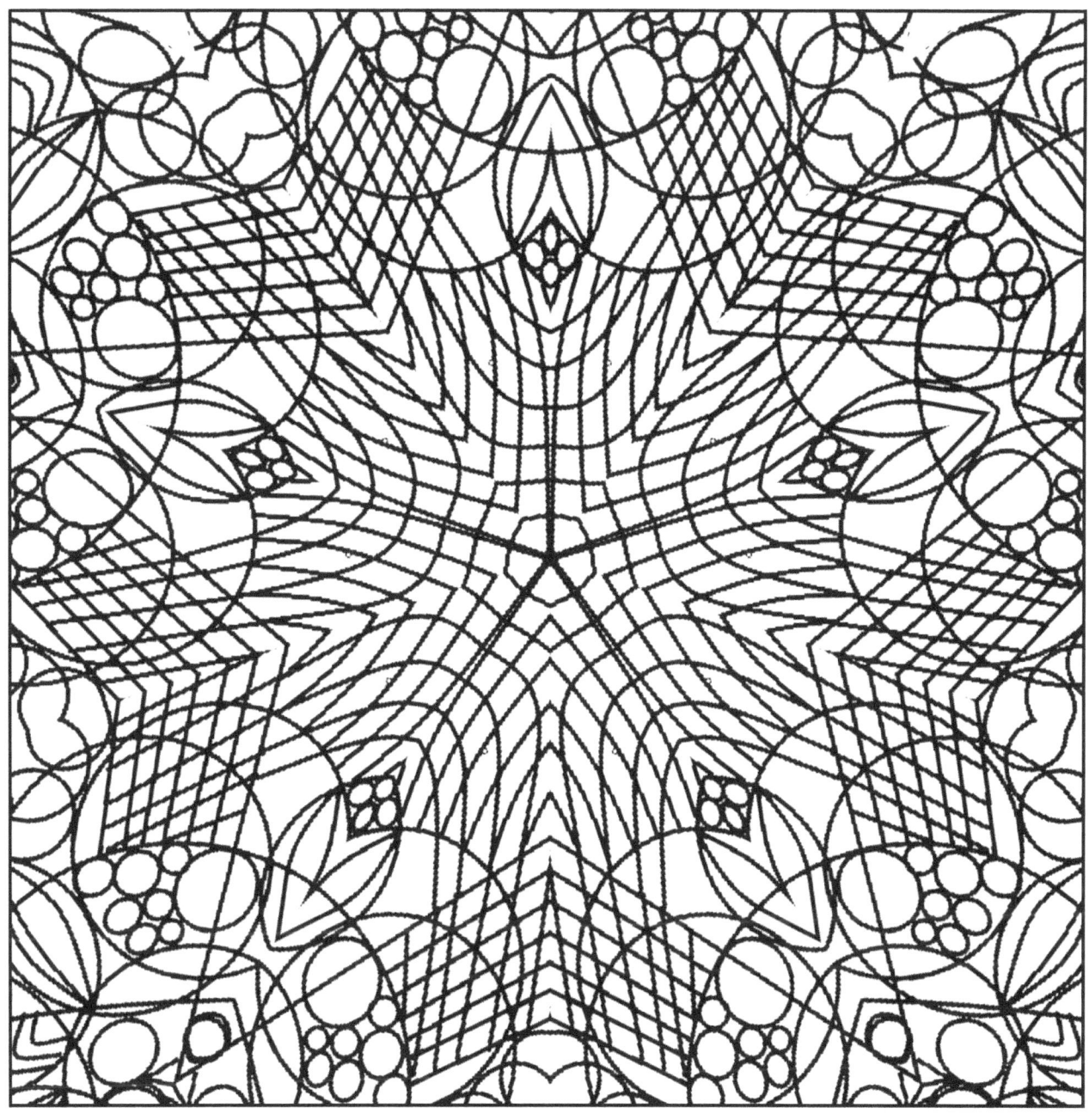

Happy Thought:

"Grief can take care of itself, but to get the full value of a joy you must have somebody to divide it with."

~~Mark Twain~~

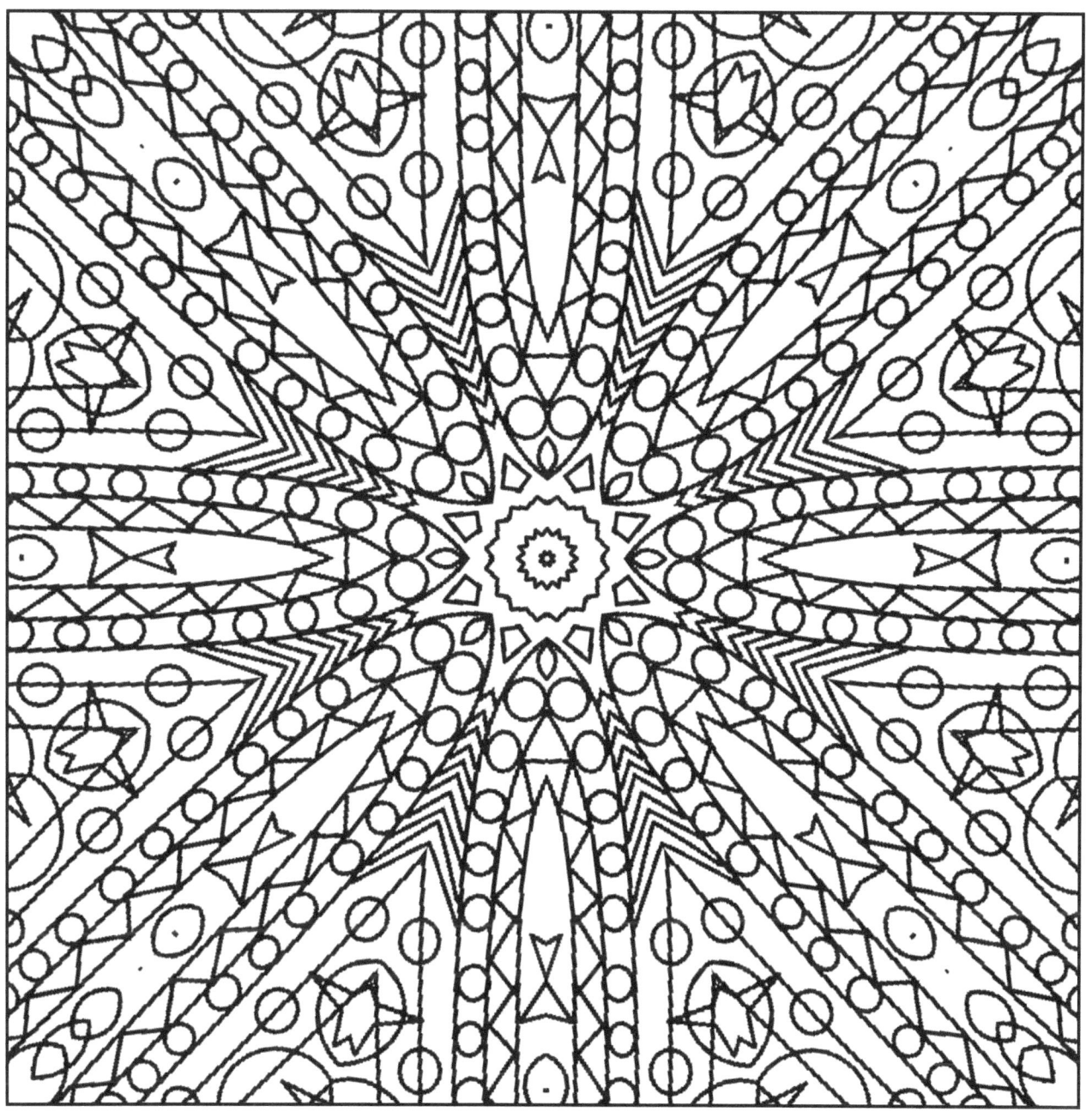

Happy Thought:

"Conquering any difficulty always gives one a secret joy, for it means pushing back a boundary-line and adding to one's liberty."

~~Henri Frederic Amiel~~

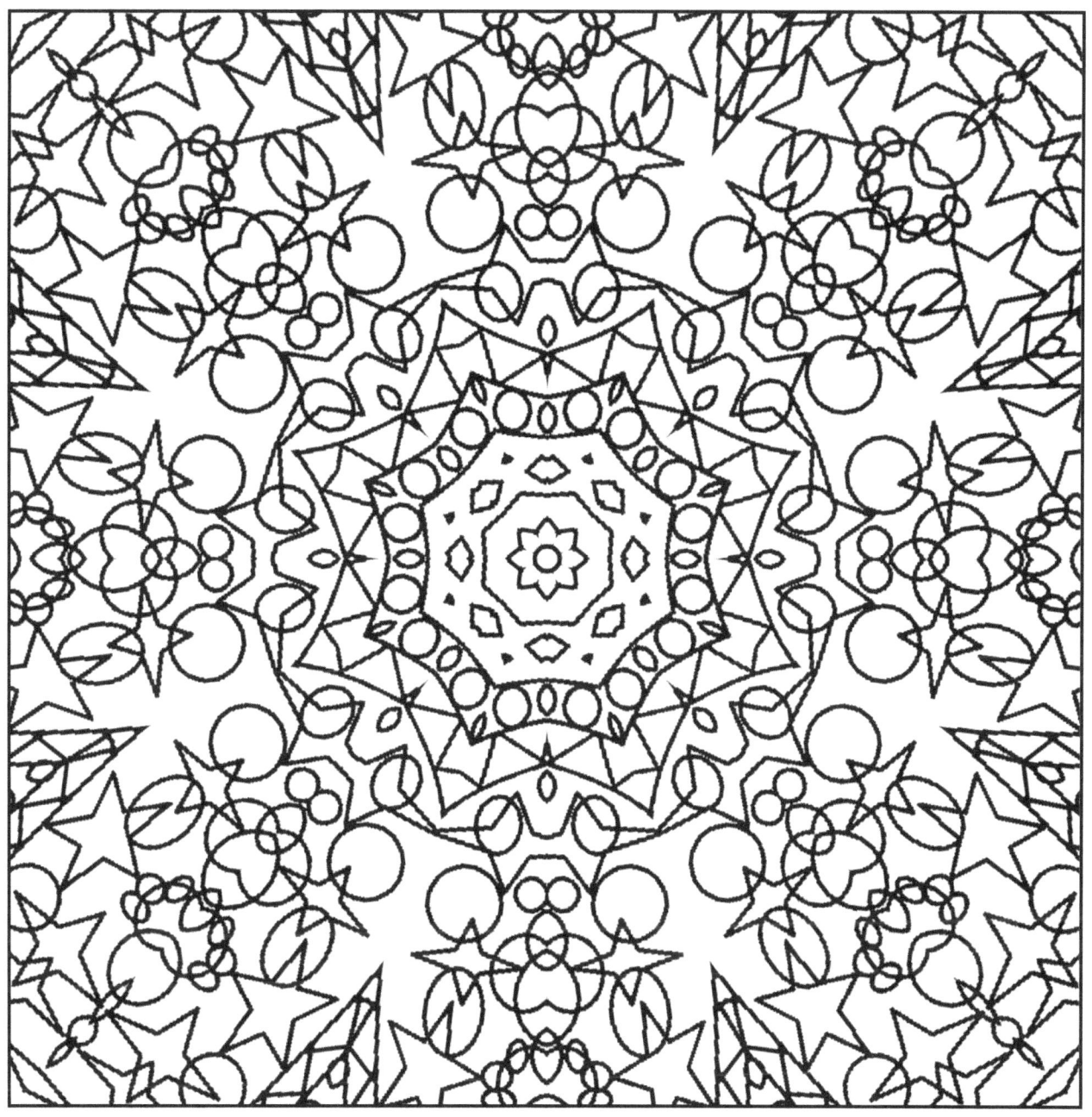

Happy Thought:

"Some of the happiest people I know have none of the things the world insists are necessary for satisfaction and joy."

~~Joseph B. Wirthlin~~

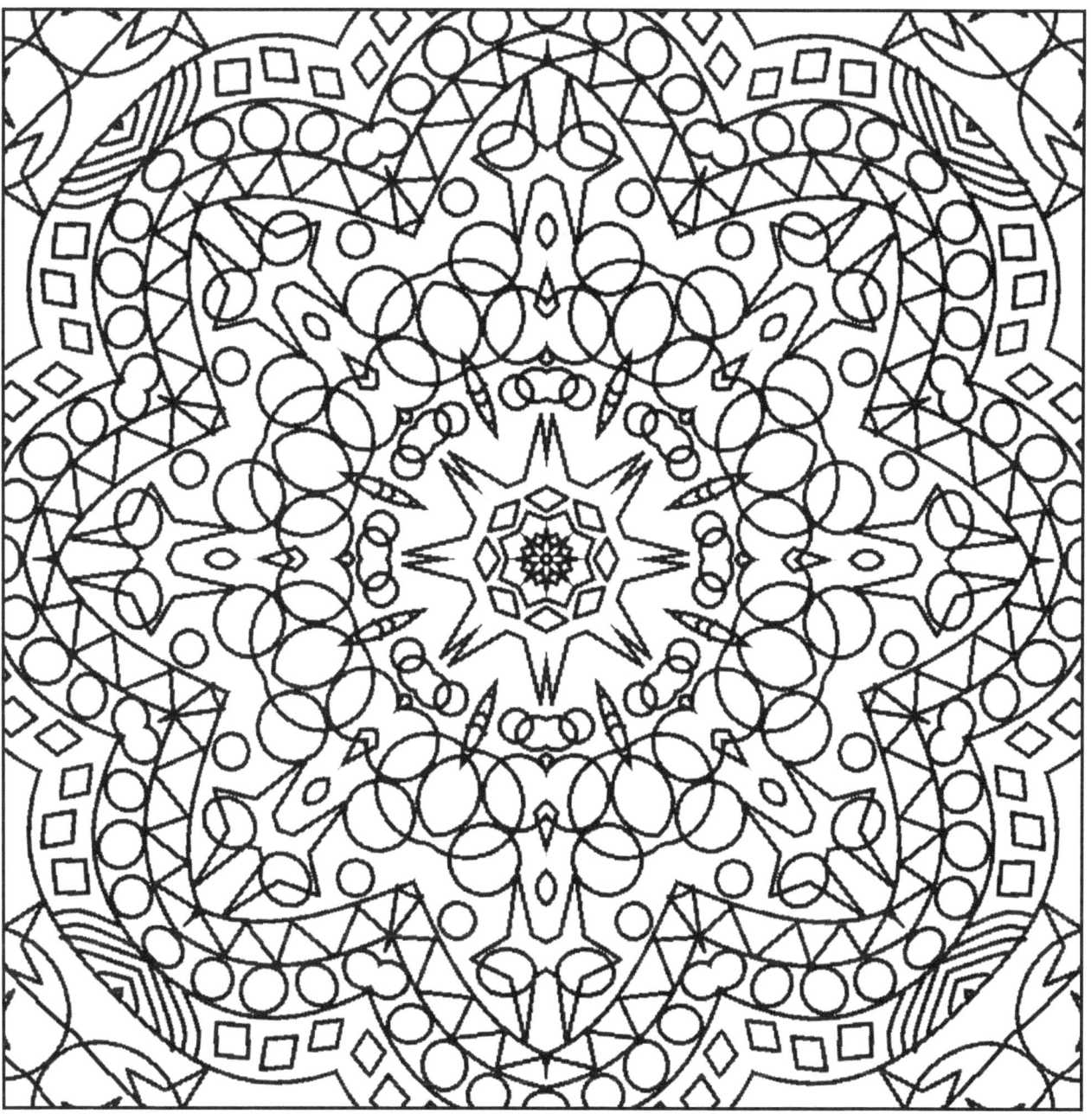

Happy Thought:

"If you so choose, each day can be filled with even more joy than the one before. If you so choose, even the most seemingly random events can work in your favor."

~~Ralph Marston~~

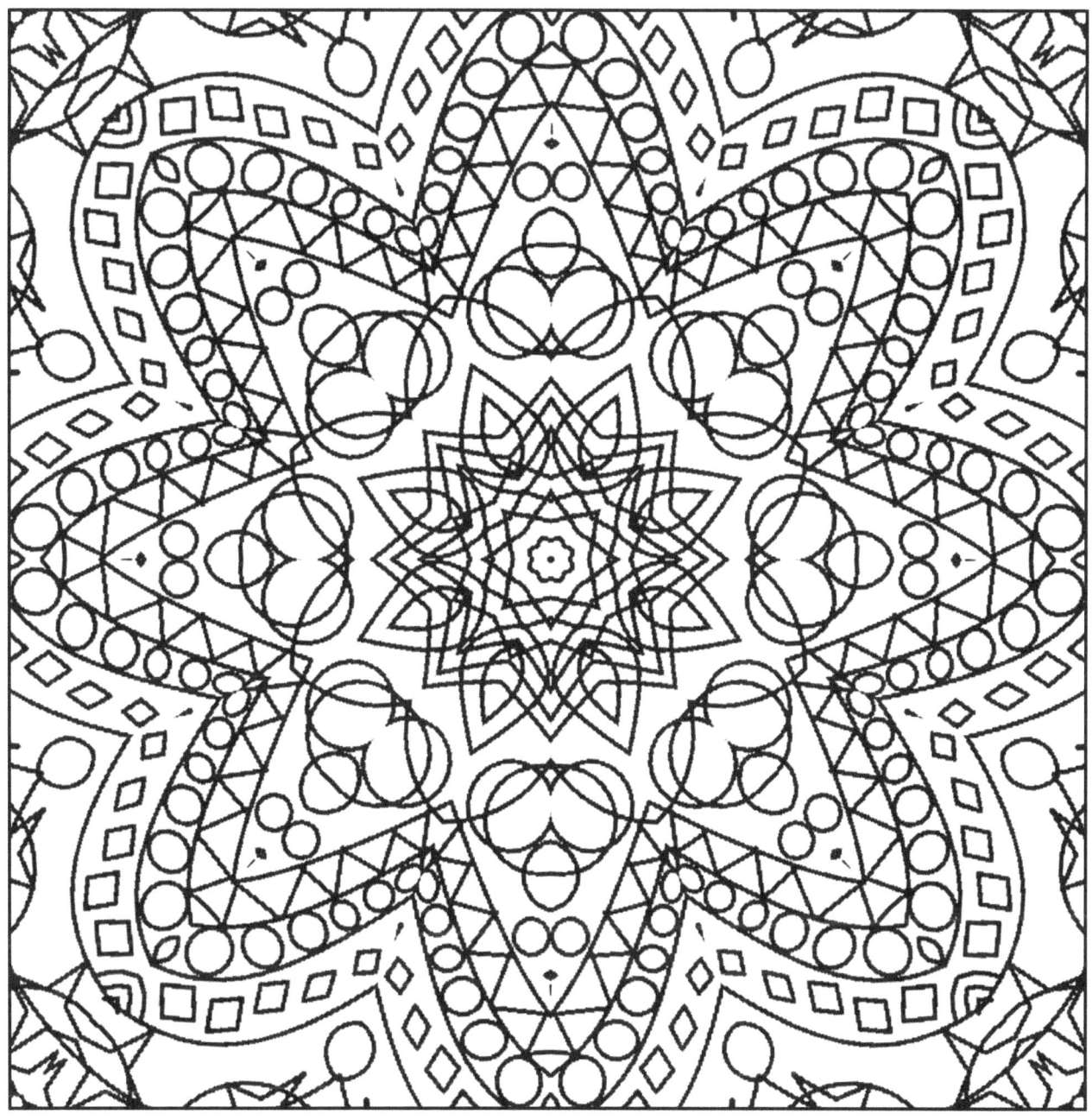

Happy Thought:

"If you really want to receive joy and happiness, then serve others with all your heart. Lift their burden, and your own burden will be lighter."

~~ Ezra Taft Benson~~

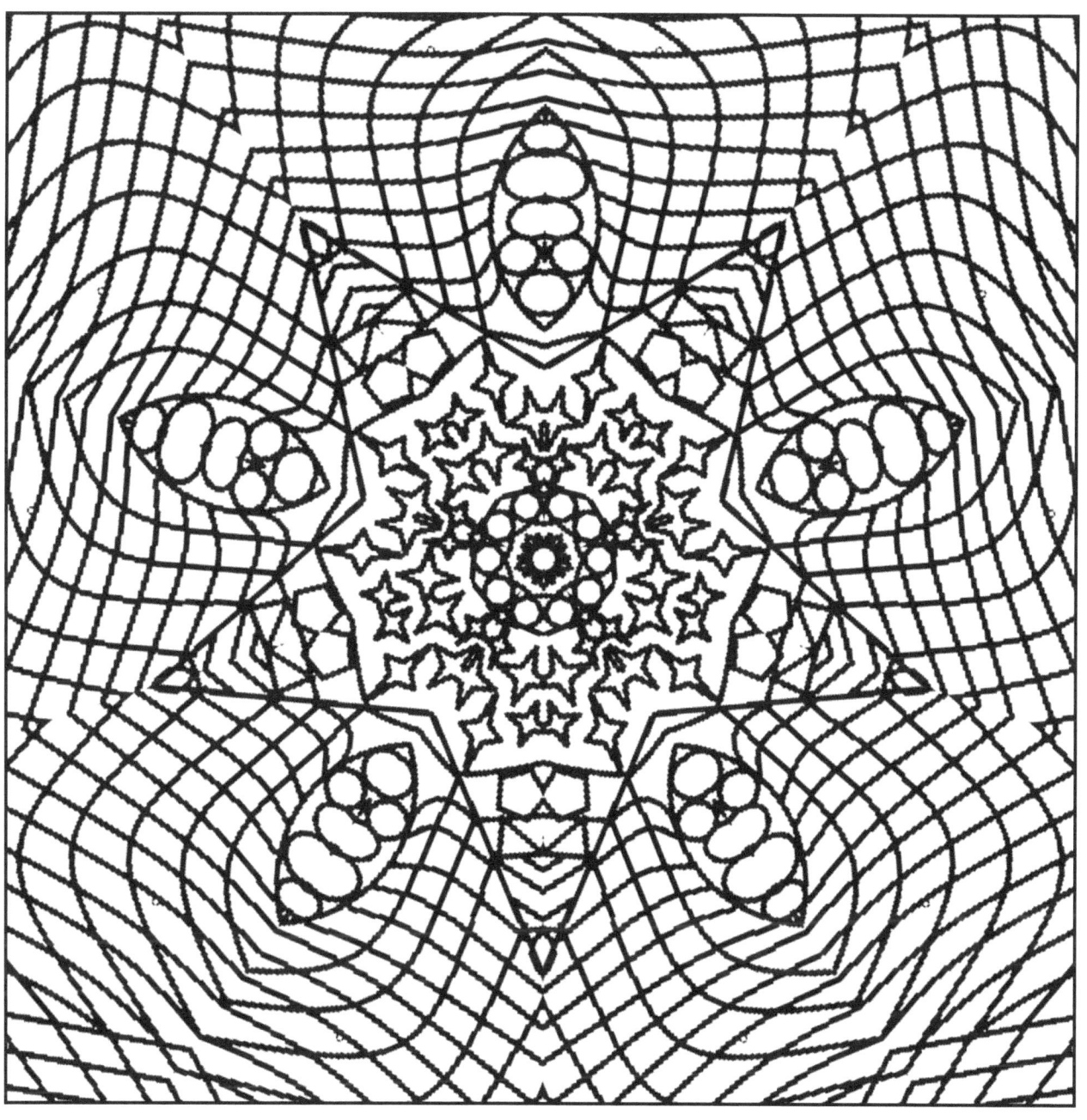

Happy Thought:

"Joy can only be real if people look upon their life as a service and have a definite object in life outside themselves and their personal happiness."

~~Leo Tolstoy~~

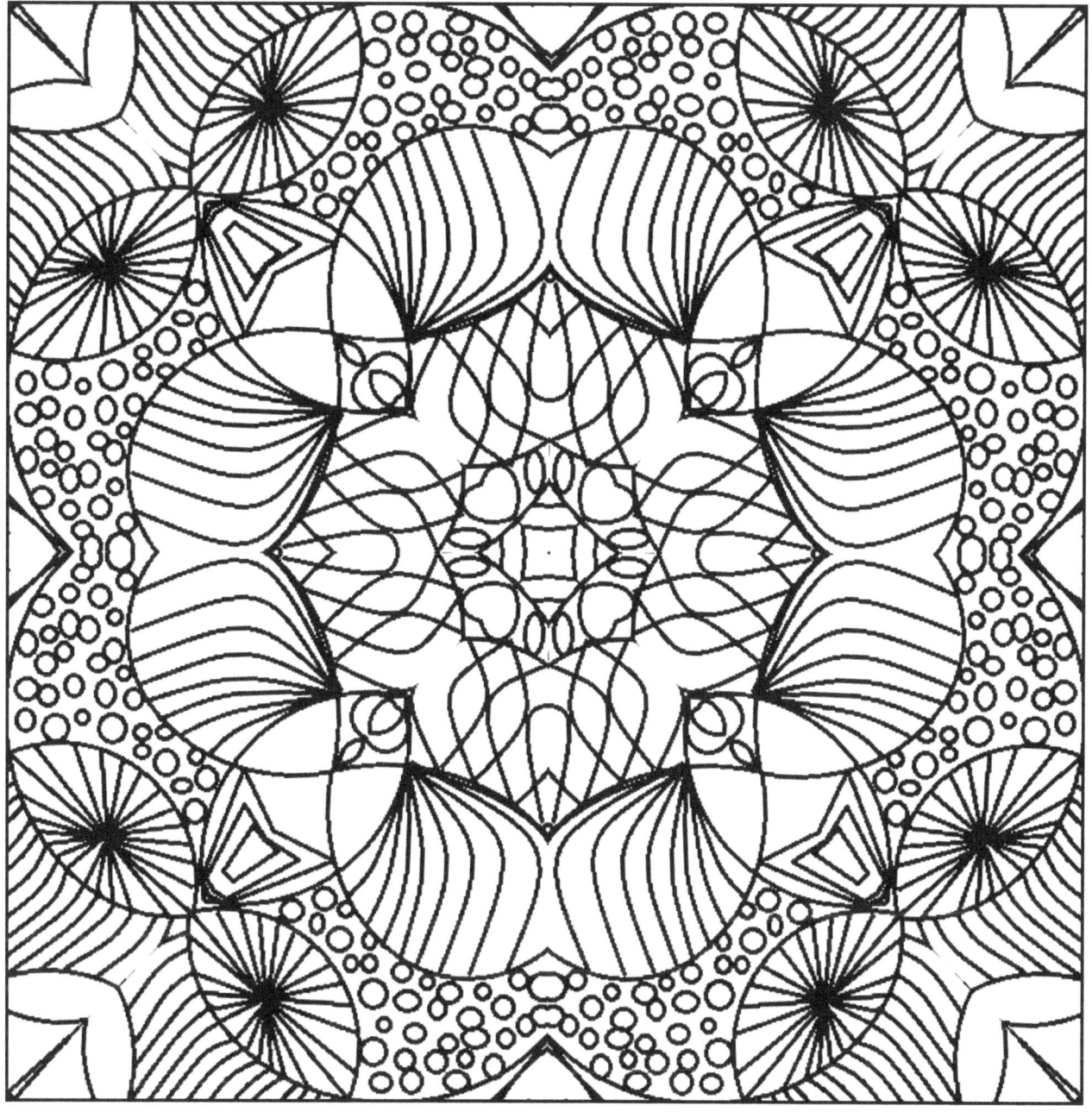

Happy Thought:

"Since you get more joy out of giving joy to others, you should put a good deal of thought into the happiness that you are able to give."

~~Eleanor Roosevelt~~

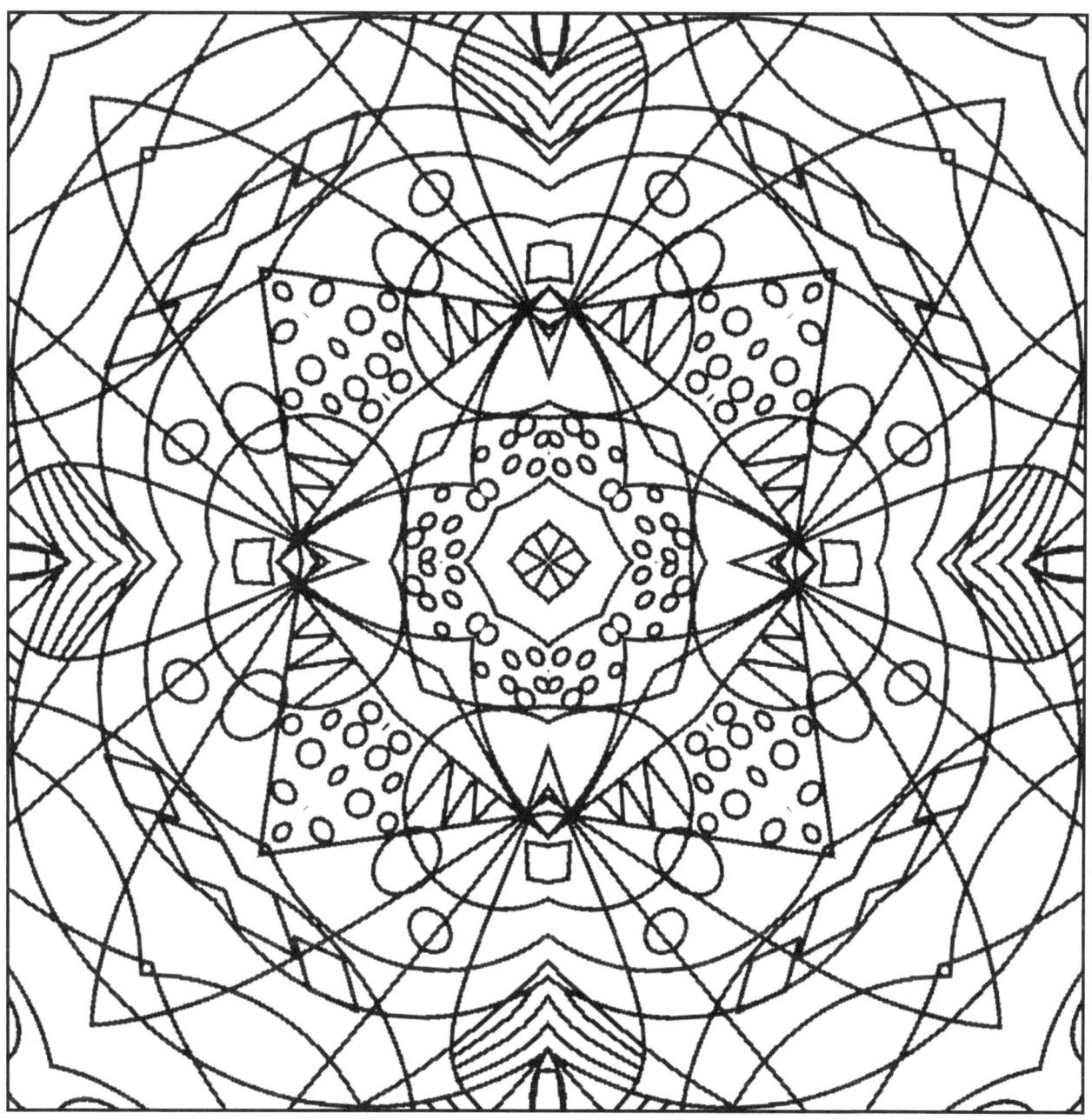

Happy Thought:

"Find joy in everything you choose to do. Every job, relationship, home...
it's your responsibility to love it, or change it."

~~Chuck Palahniuk~~

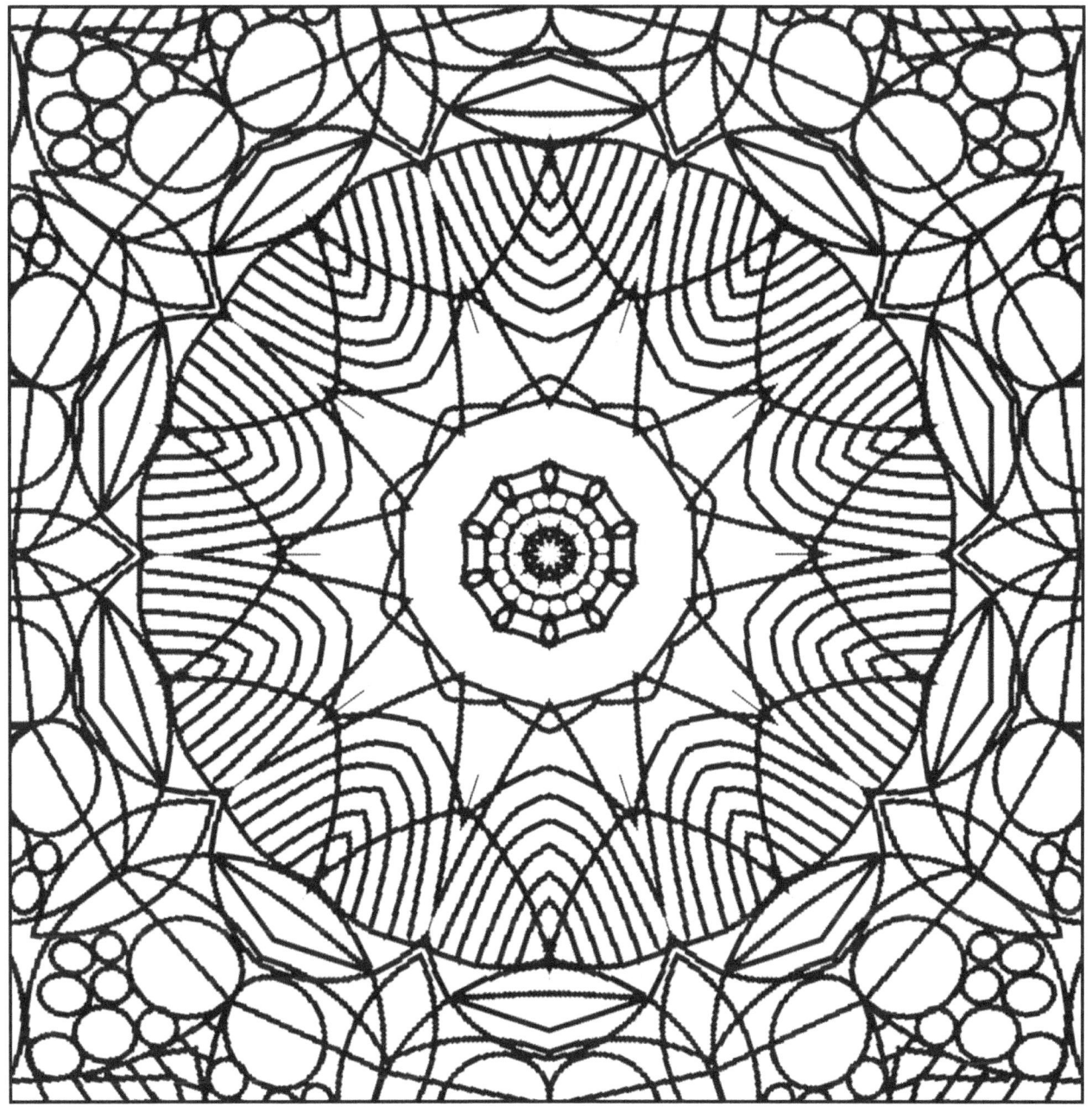

Happy Thought:

"The sun does not shine for a few trees and flowers, but for the wide world's joy."

~~Henry Ward Beecher~~

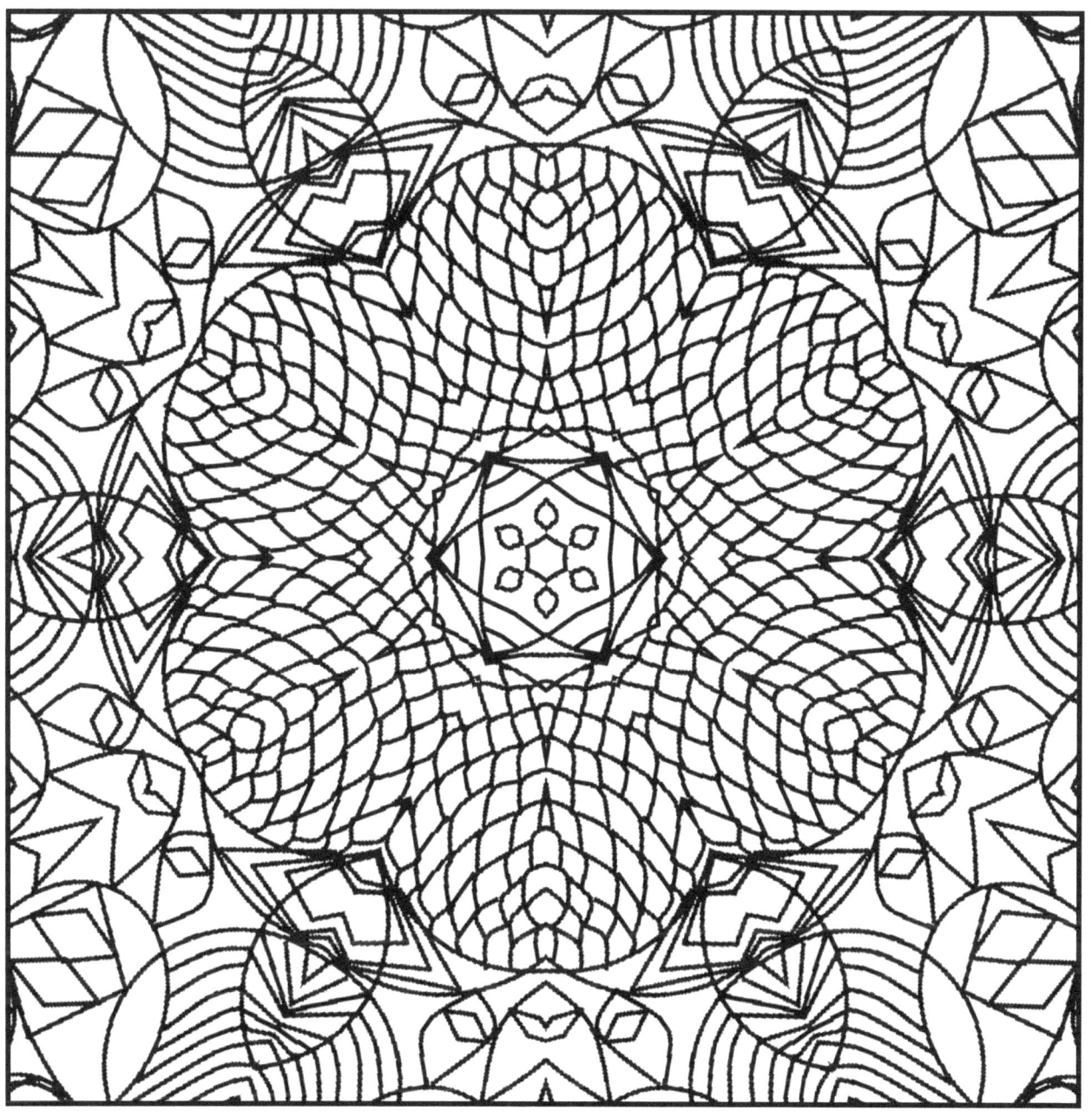

Happy Thought:

"Simplicity, clarity, singleness: These are the attributes that give our lives power and vividness and joy as they are also the marks of great art. They seem to be the purpose of God for his whole creation."

~~Richard Holloway~~

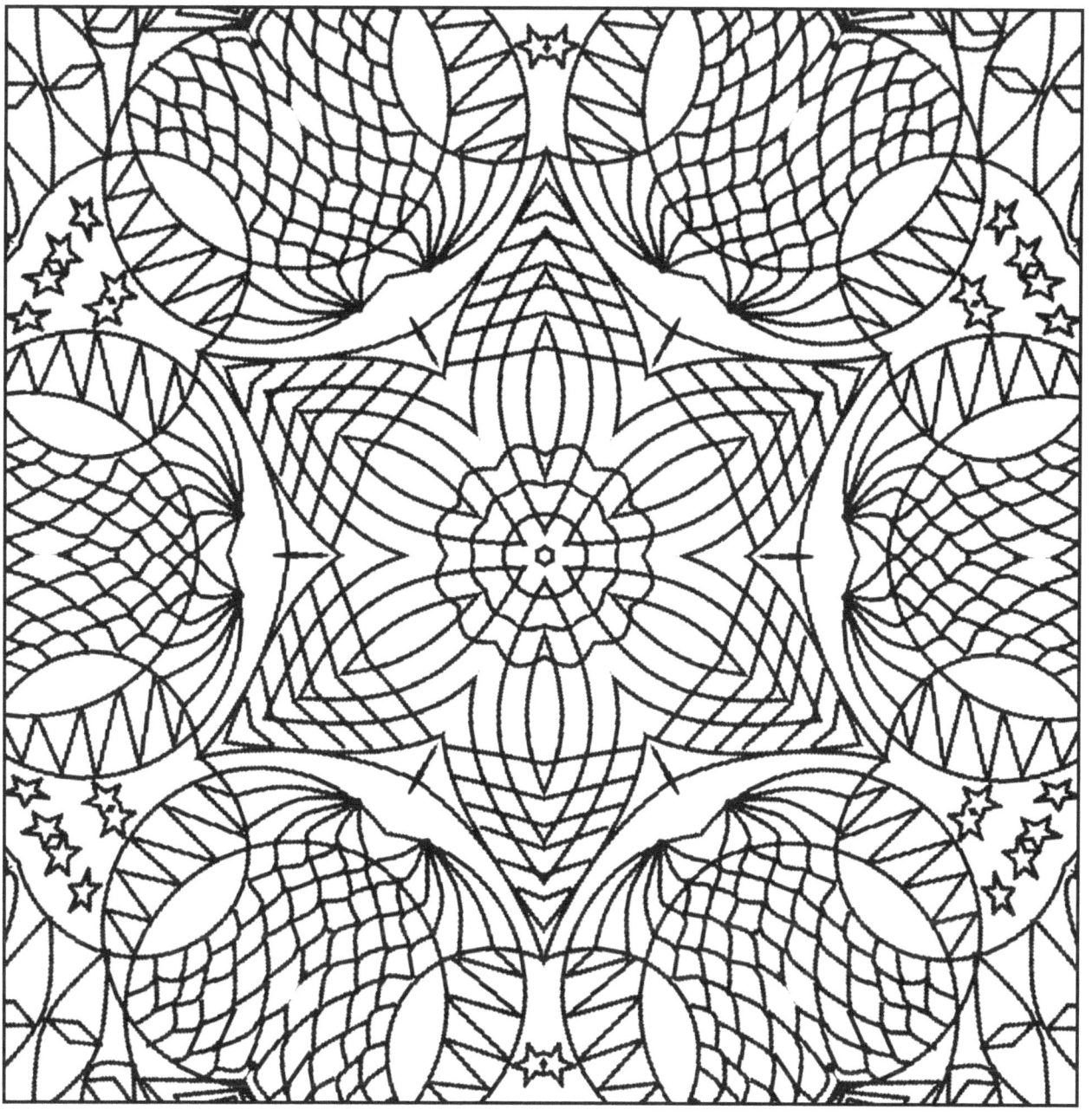

Happy Thought:

"The secret of joy in work is contained in one word - excellence. To know how to do something well is to enjoy it."

~~ Pearl S. Buck~~

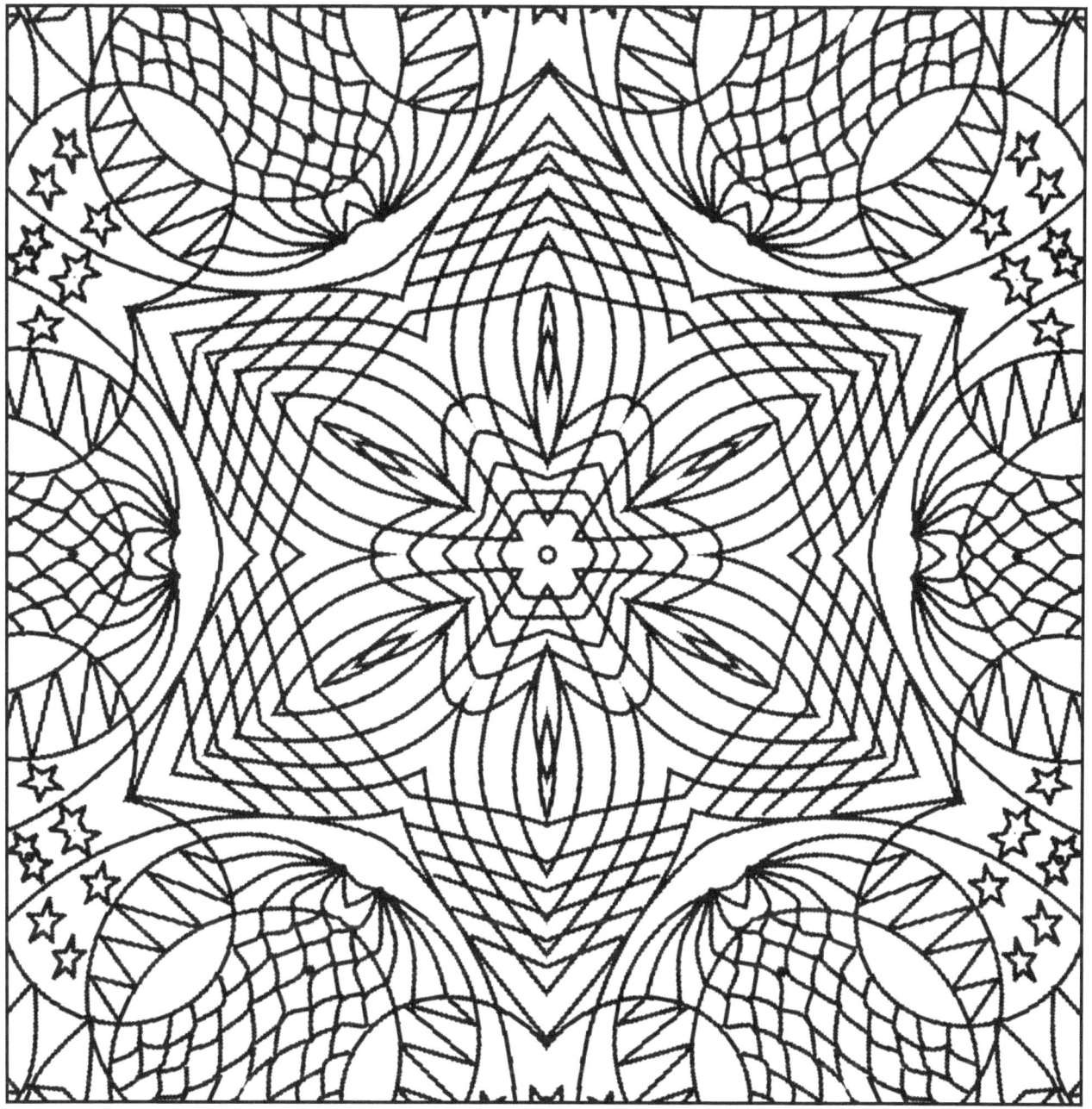

Happy Thought:

"Hope is a state of mind, not of the world. Hope, in this deep and powerful sense, is not the same as joy that things are going well, or willingness to invest in enterprises that are obviously heading for success, but rather an ability to work for something because it is good."

~~Vaclav Havel~~

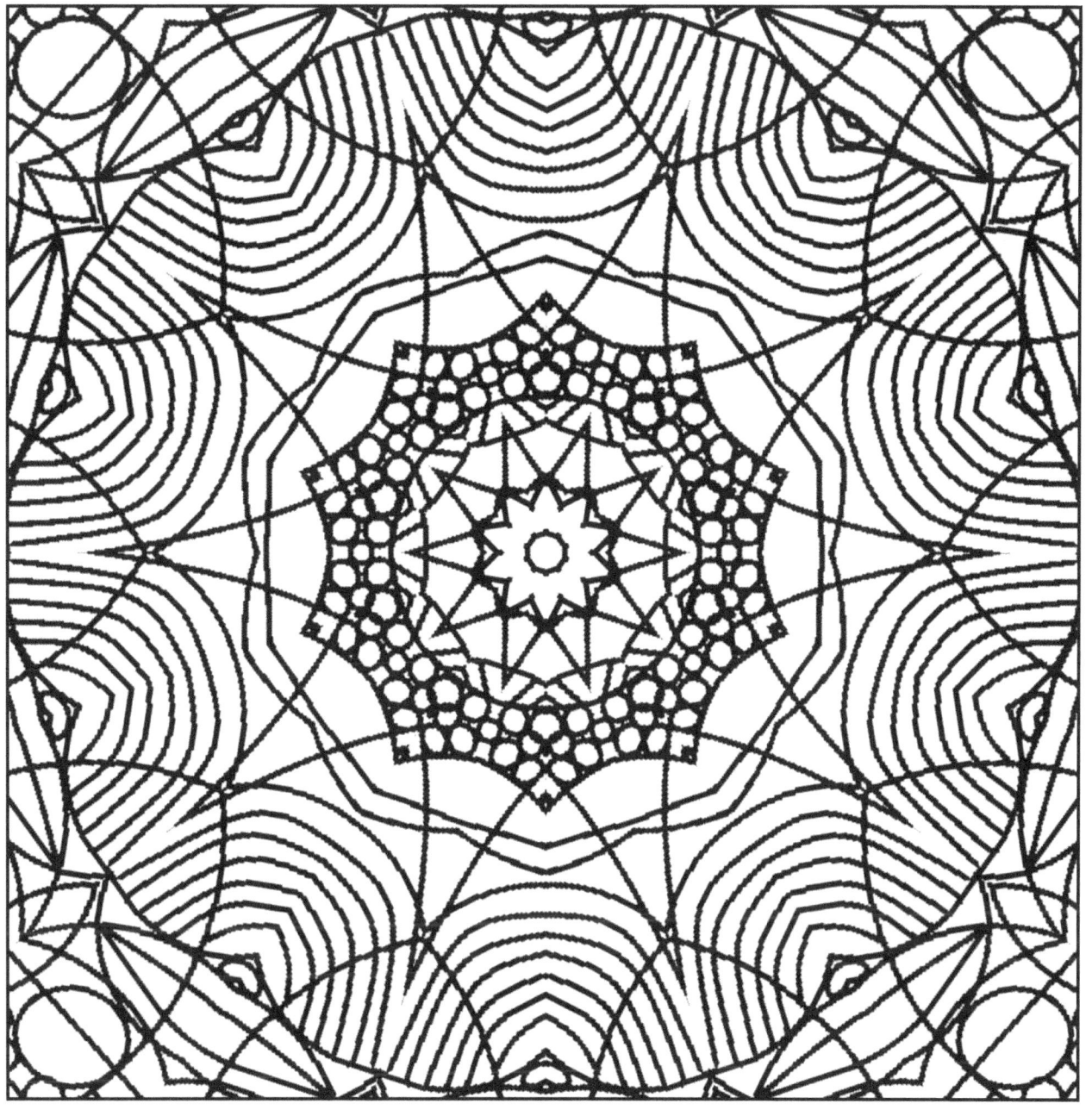

Happy Thought:

"Sometimes your joy is the source of your smile, but sometimes your smile can be the source of your joy.

~~Nhat Hanh~~

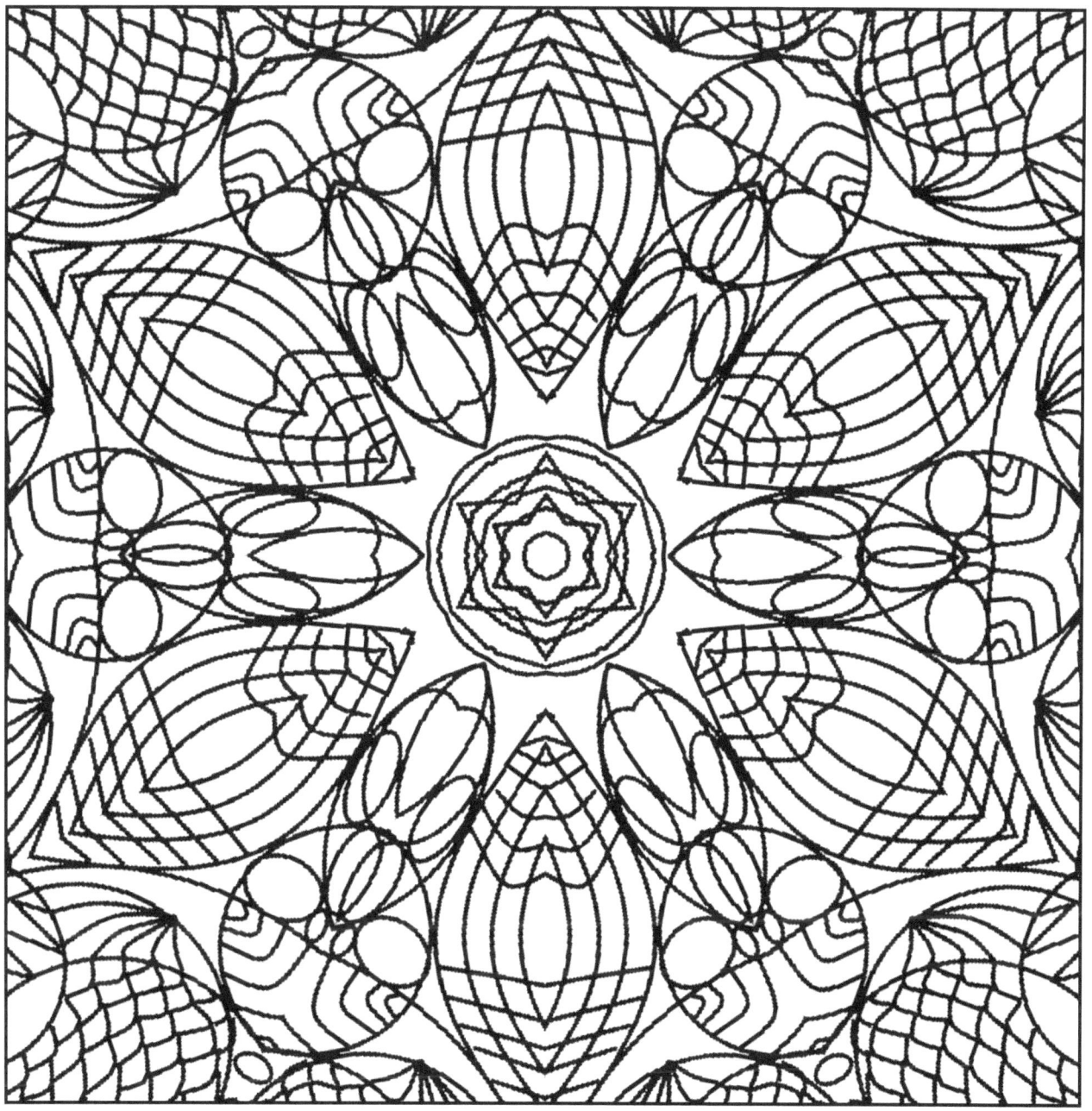

Happy Thought:

"Disappointment is a sticky one, because no one can steal contentment, joy, gratitude, or peace - we have to give it away."

~~Kristin Armstrong

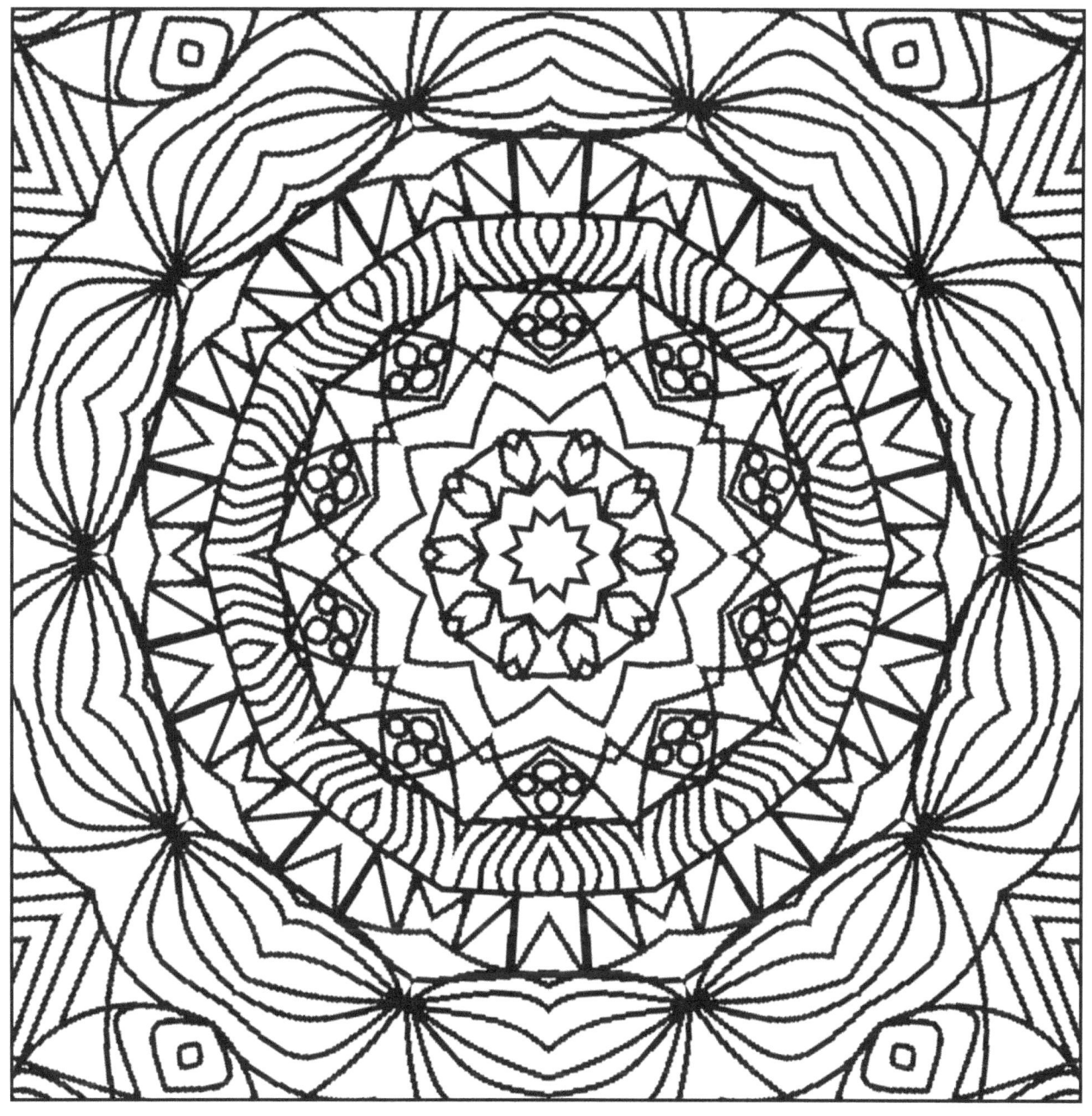

Happy Thought:

"Through loyalty to the past, our mind refuses to realize that tomorrow's joy is possible only if today's makes way for it; that each wave owes the beauty of its line only to the withdrawal of the preceding one."

~~Andre Gide~~

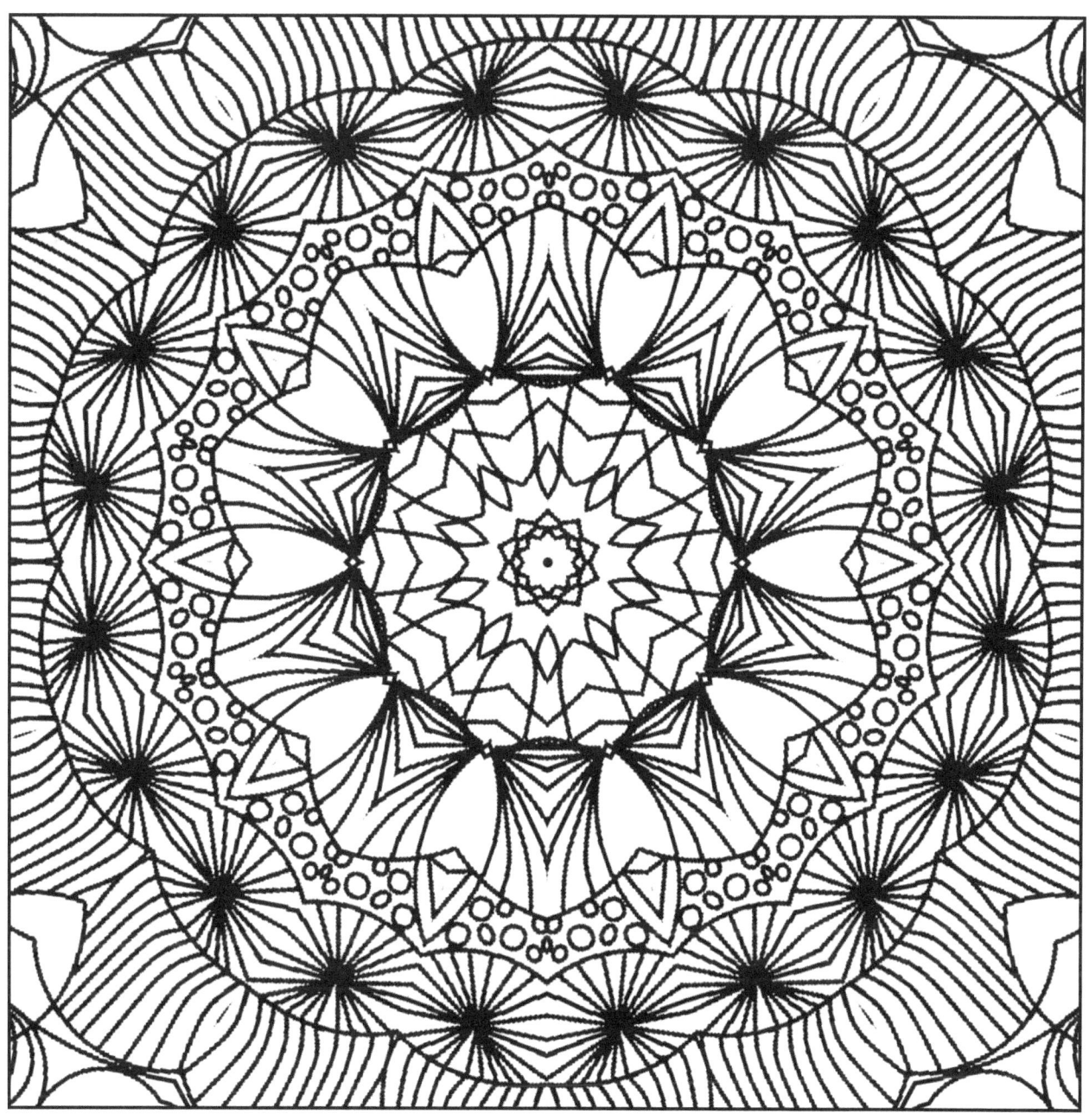

Happy Thought:

"Pleasure usually takes the form of 'me and now'; joy is 'us and always'."

~~Marvin J. Ashton~~

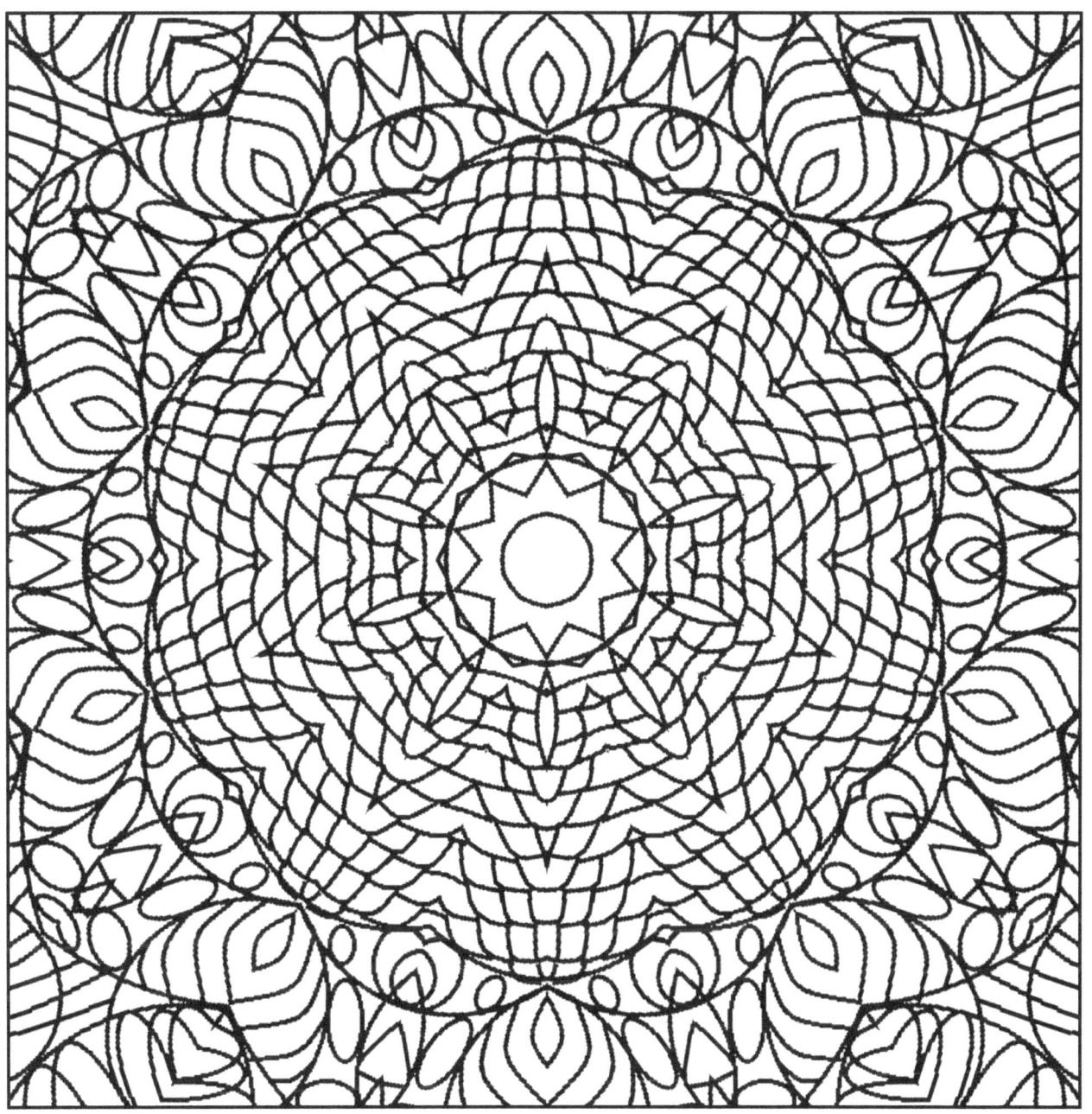

Happy Thought:

"There are those who give with joy, and that joy is their reward."

~~Khalil Gibran~~

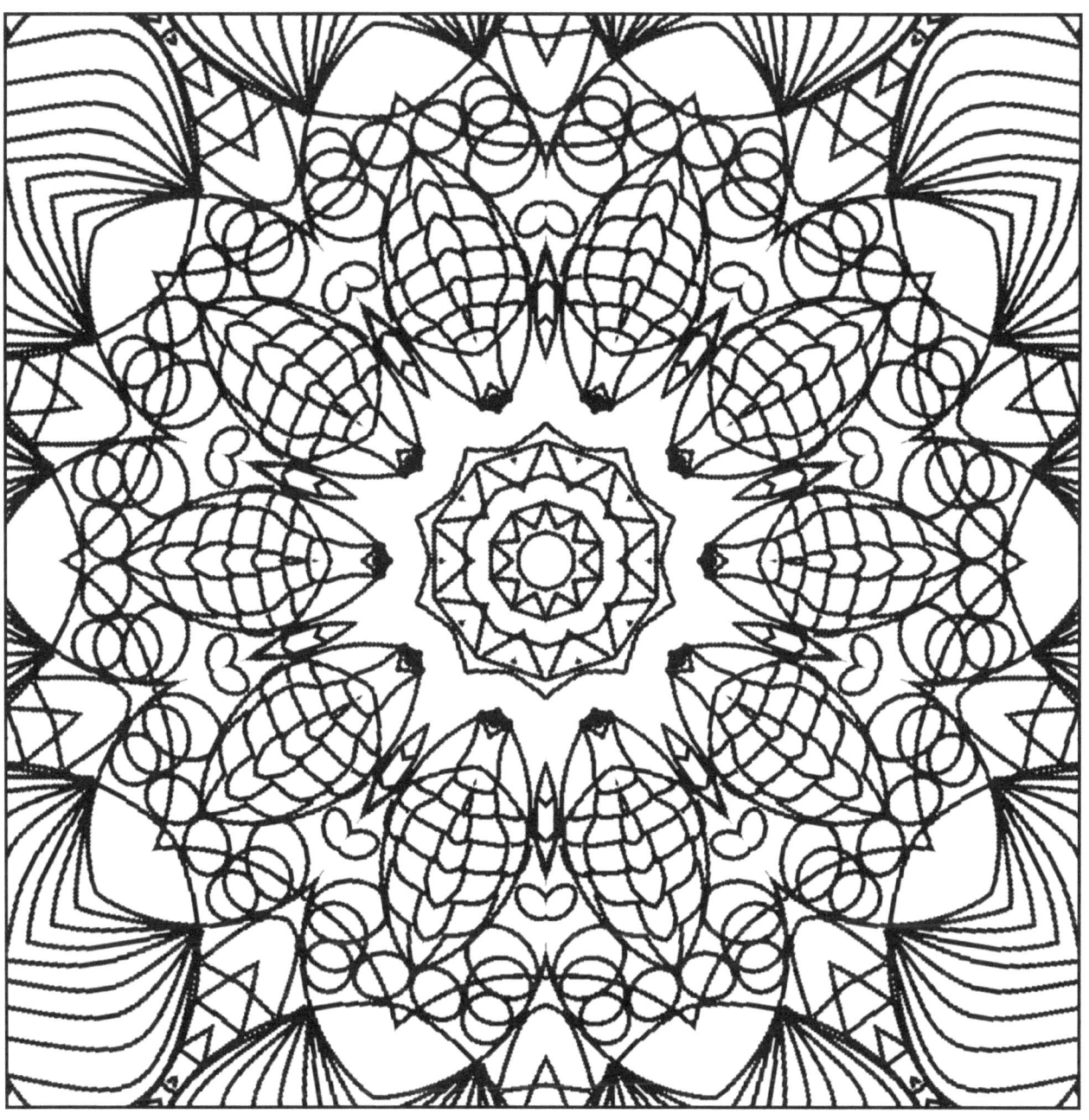

Happy Thought:

"I think we manifest the very thing we put out. If you're putting out negativity, then you're going to retrieve that same sentiment. If you emanate joy, it comes back to you."

~~Robin Wright~~

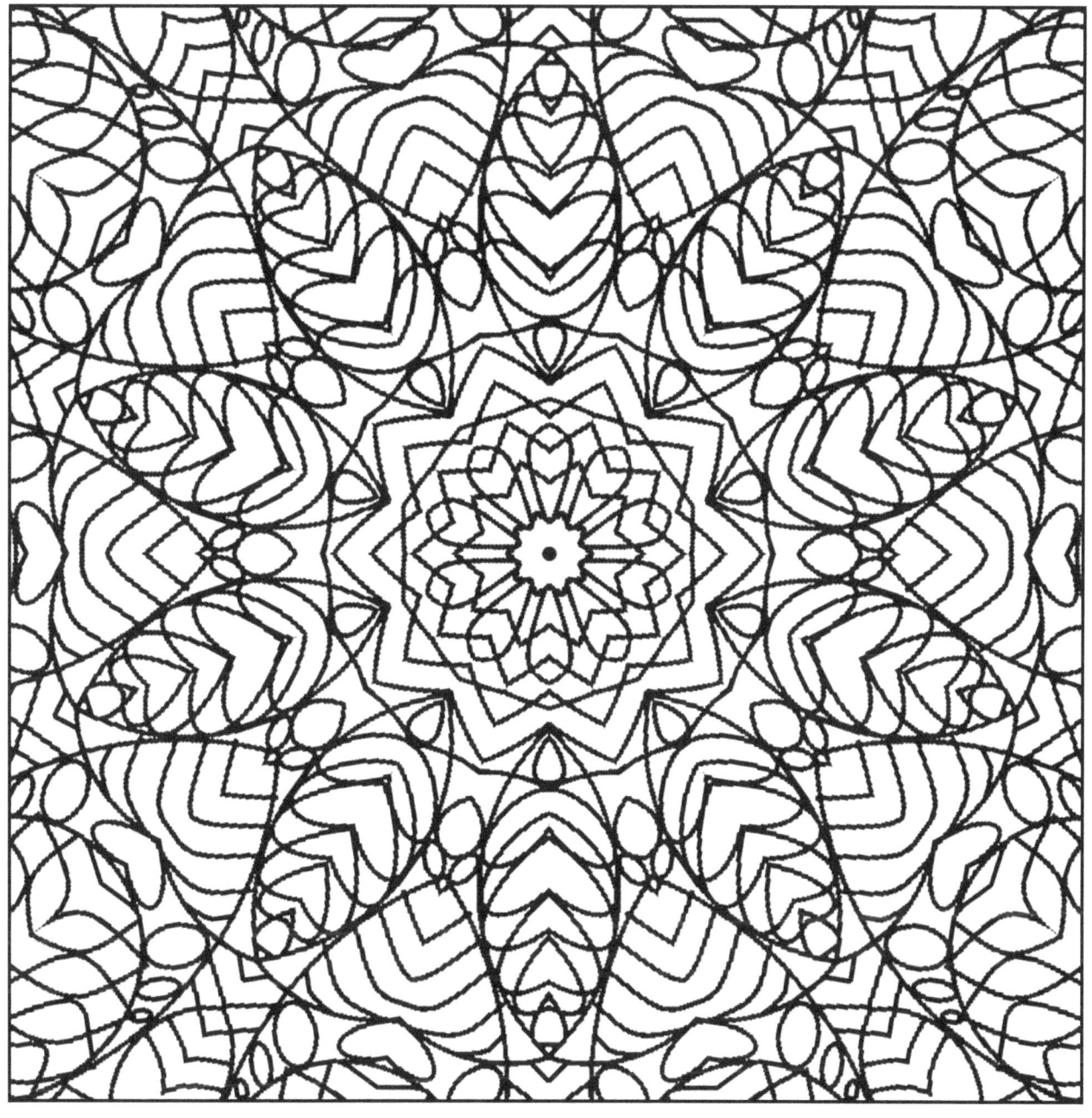

Happy Thought:

"We all find joy and radiance and a reason to move on even in the most dire of circumstances. Even in chaos and madness, there's still a beauty that comes from just the vibrancy of another human spirit."

~~Ishmael Beah~~

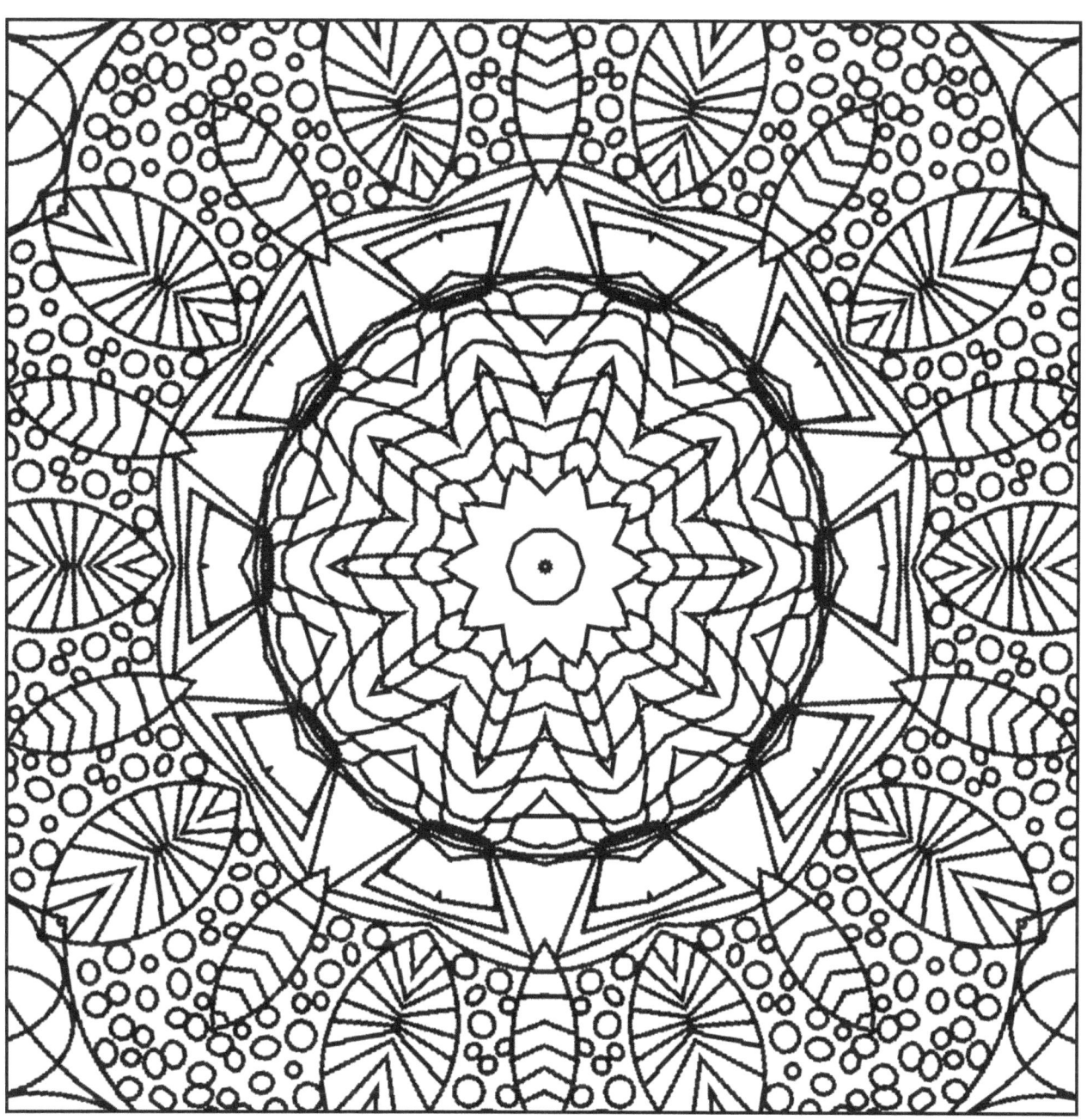

Happy Thoughts

"Your joy comes from how you think, the choices that we make in life."

~~Joyce Meyer~~

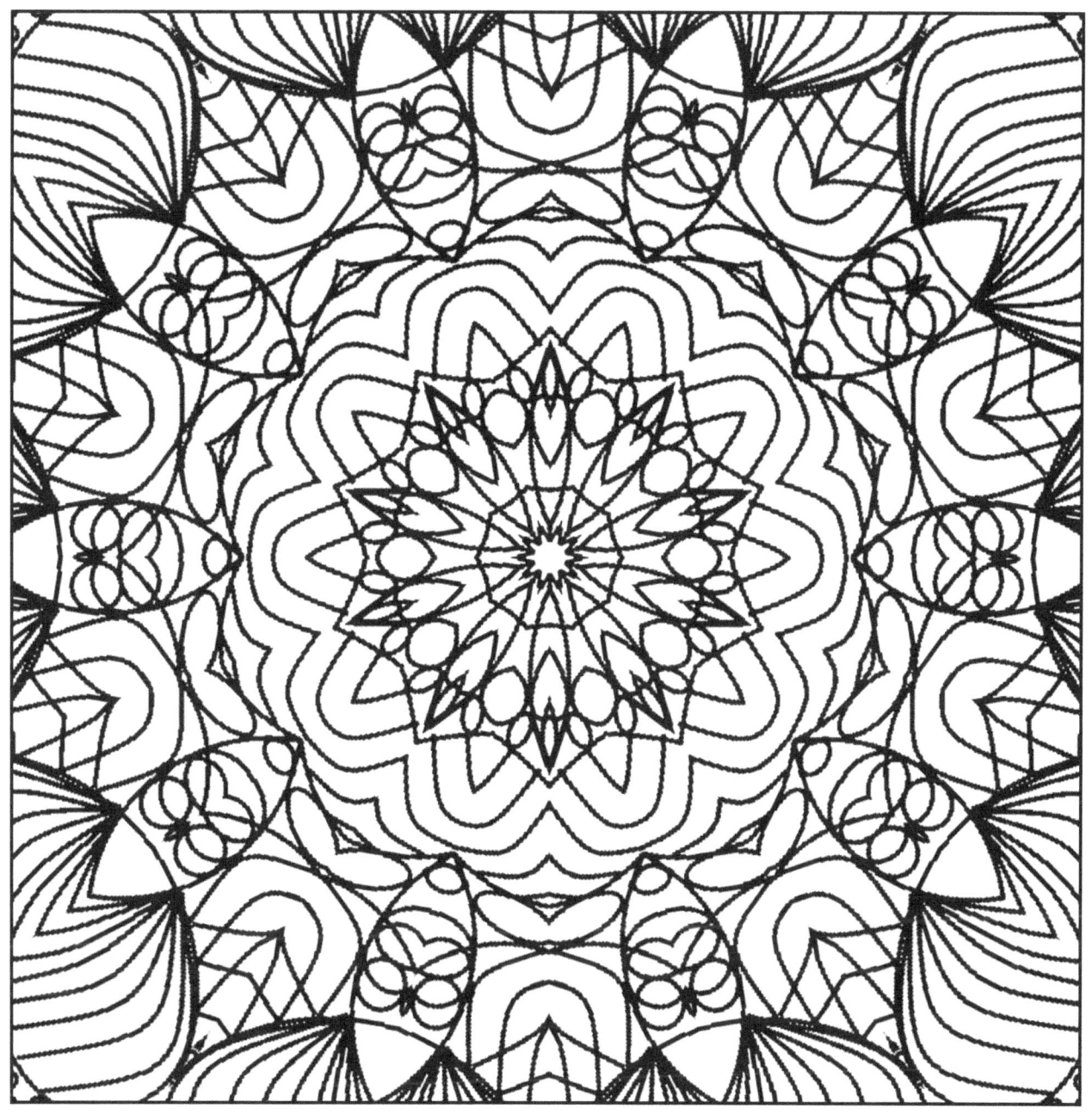

Happy Thought:

"Instead of asking 'How much damage will the work in question bring about?' why not ask 'How much good? How much joy?'"

~~Henry Miller~~

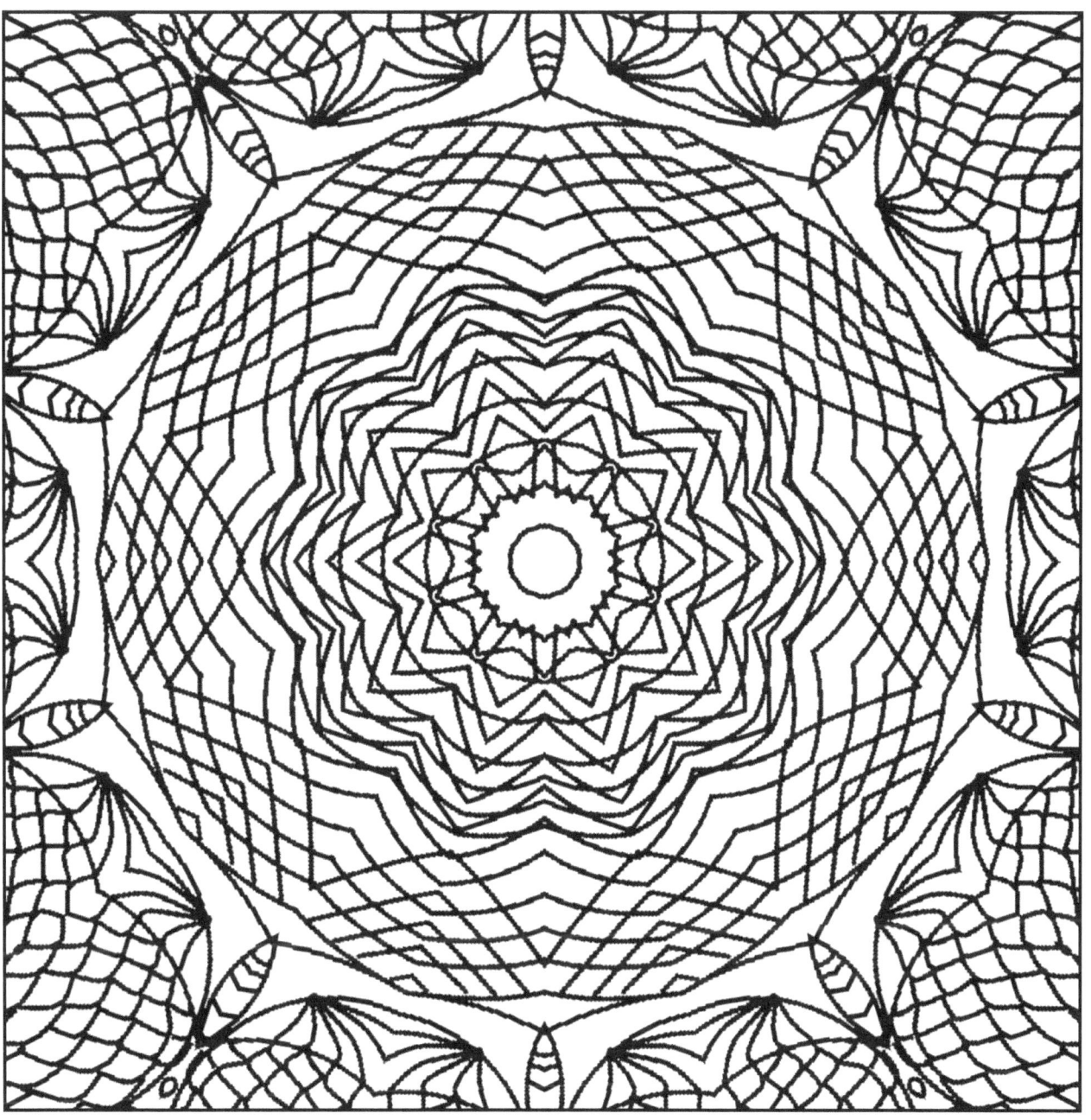

Happy Thoughts:

"What we get from this adventure is just sheer joy. And joy is, after all, the end of life. We do not live to eat and make money."

~~George Leigh Mallory~~

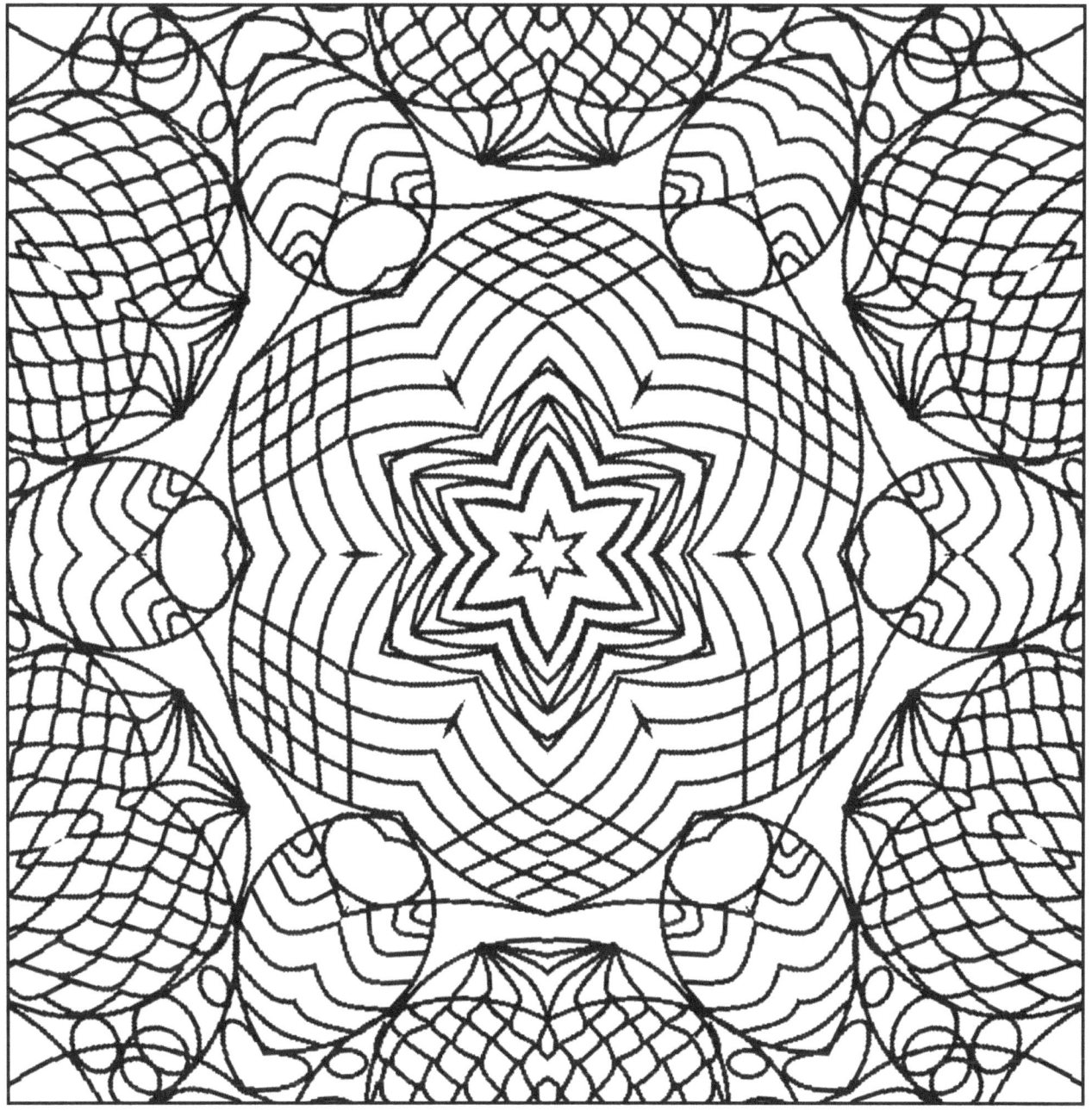

Happy Thought:

"Each child brings so much joy and hope into the world, and that is reason enough for being here. As you grow older, you will contribute something else to this world, and only you can discover what that is."

~~Sharon Creech~~

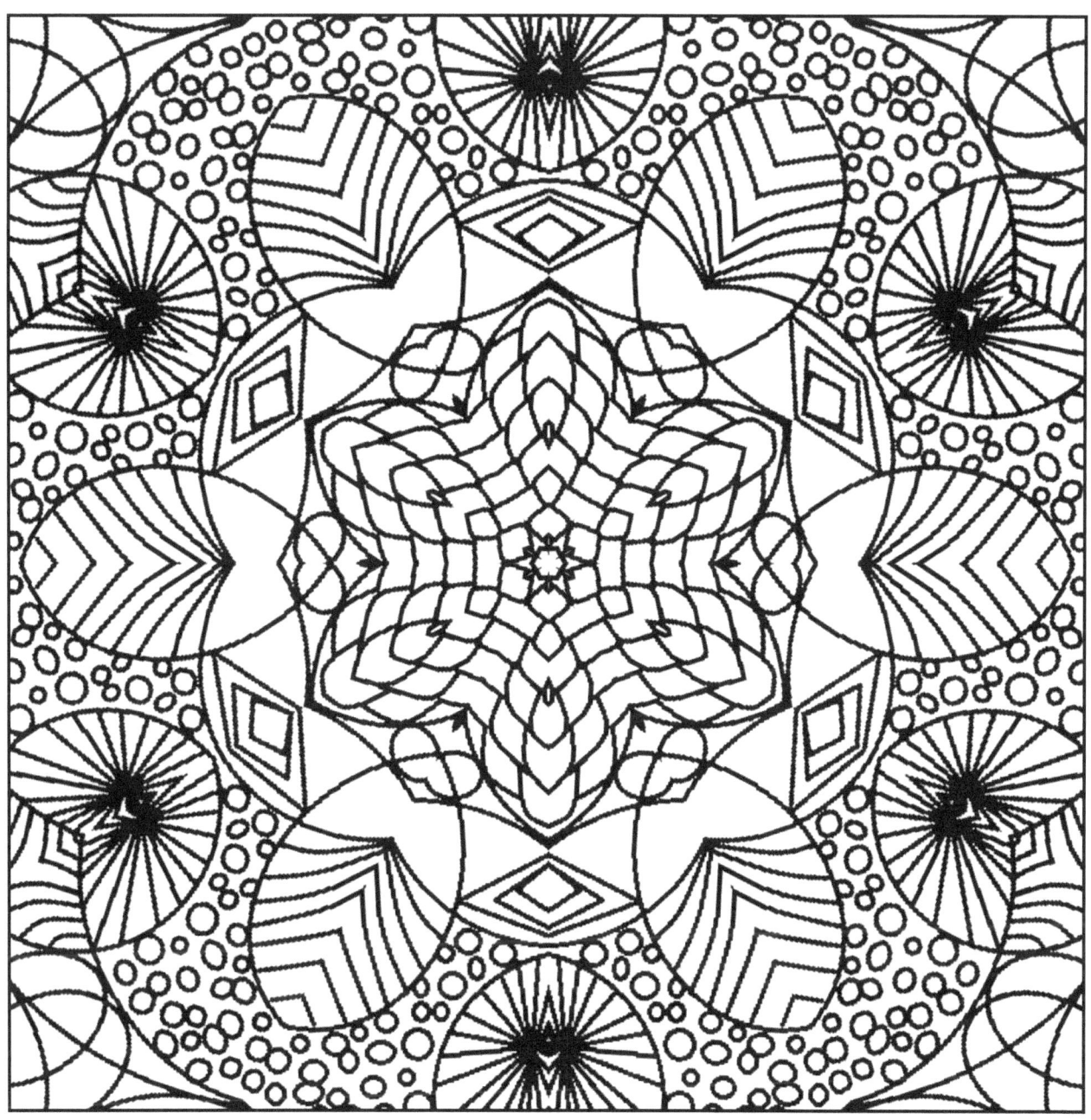

Happy Thought:

"If you do a good job for others, you heal yourself at the same time, because a dose of joy is a spiritual cure. It transcends all barriers."

~~Ed Sullivan~~

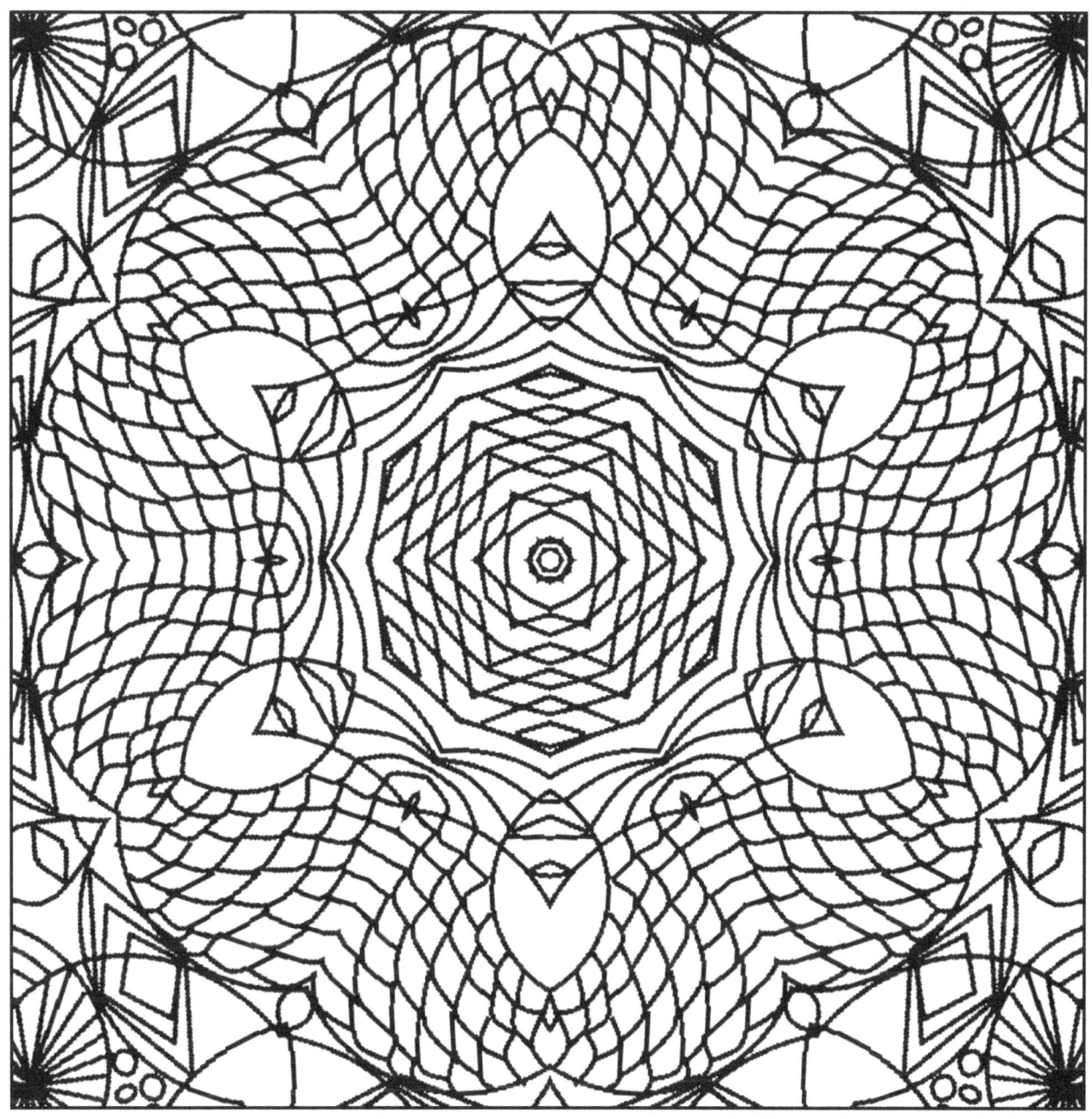

Happy Thought:

"Joy of living is sustainable; fear of dying is not."

~~Dean Ornish~~

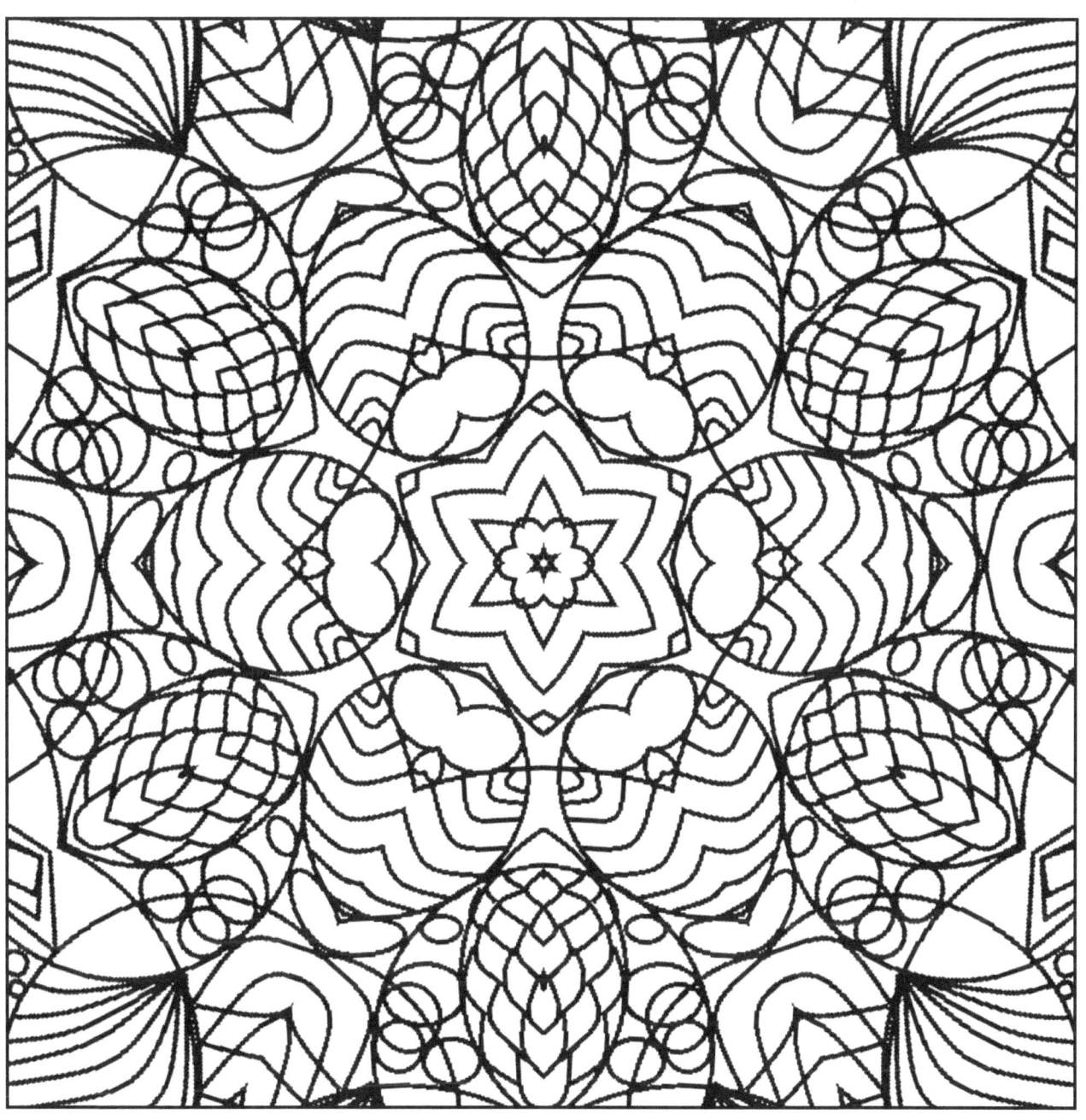

Happy Thought:

"Joy is a subtle elf; I think one's happiest when he forgets himself."

~~Cyril Tourneur~~

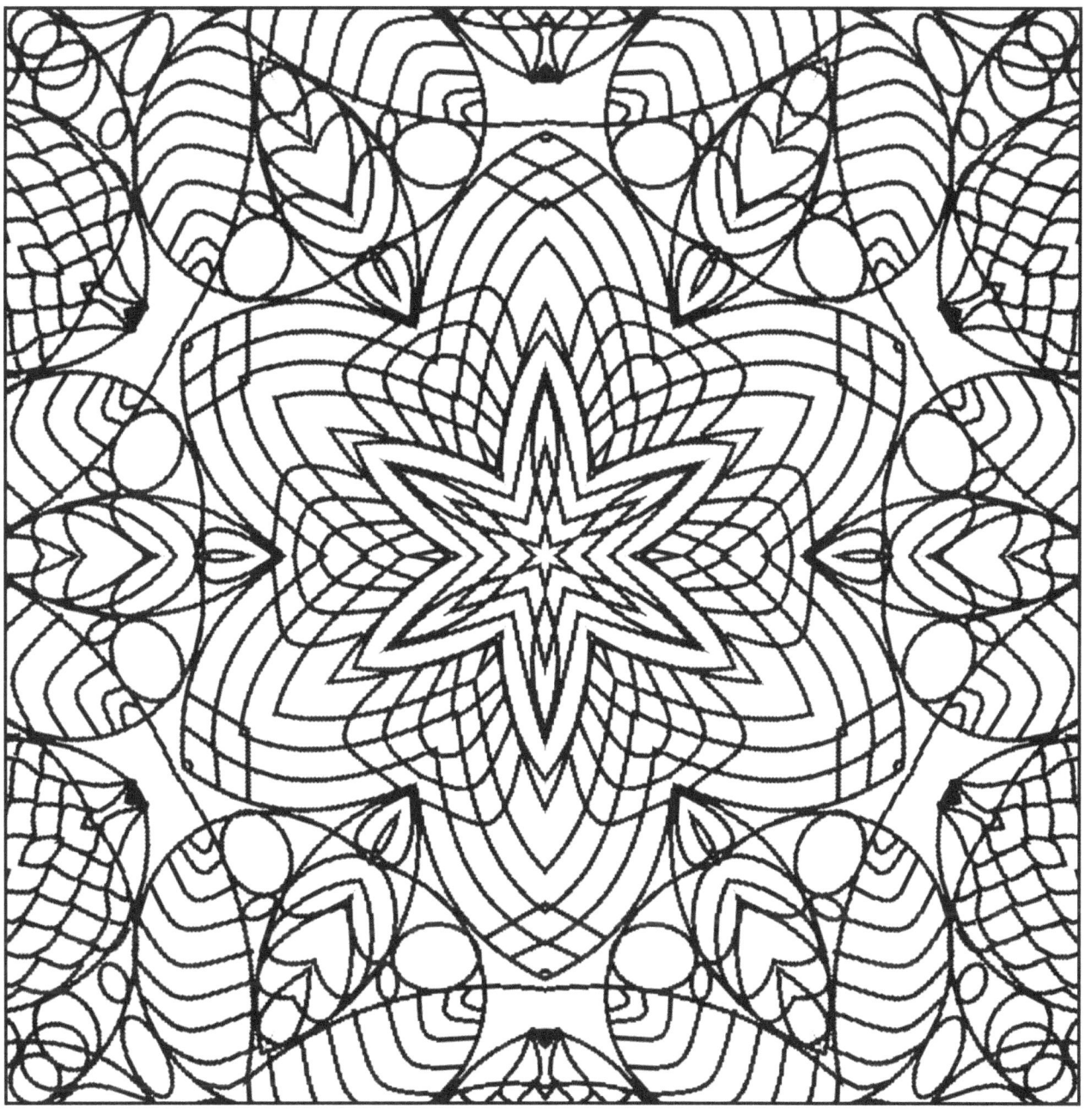

Happy Thought:

"Then there is a still higher type of courage - the courage to brave pain, to live with it, to never let others know of it and to still find joy in life; to wake up in the morning with an enthusiasm for the day ahead."

~~Howard Cosell~~

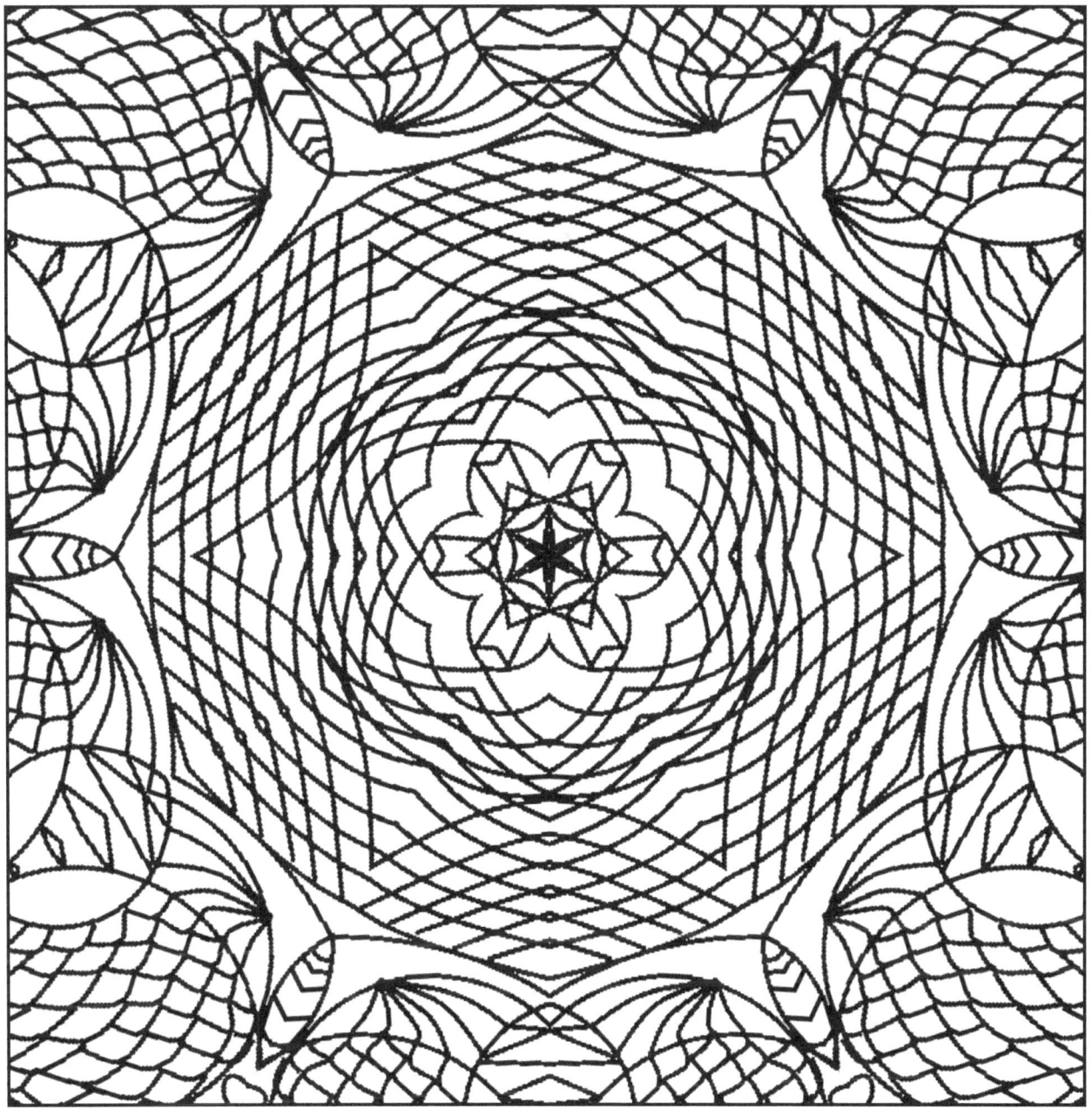

Happy Thought:

"I am probably the most selfish man you will ever meet in your life. No one gets the satisfaction or the joy that I get out of seeing kids realize there is hope."

~~Jerry Lewis~~

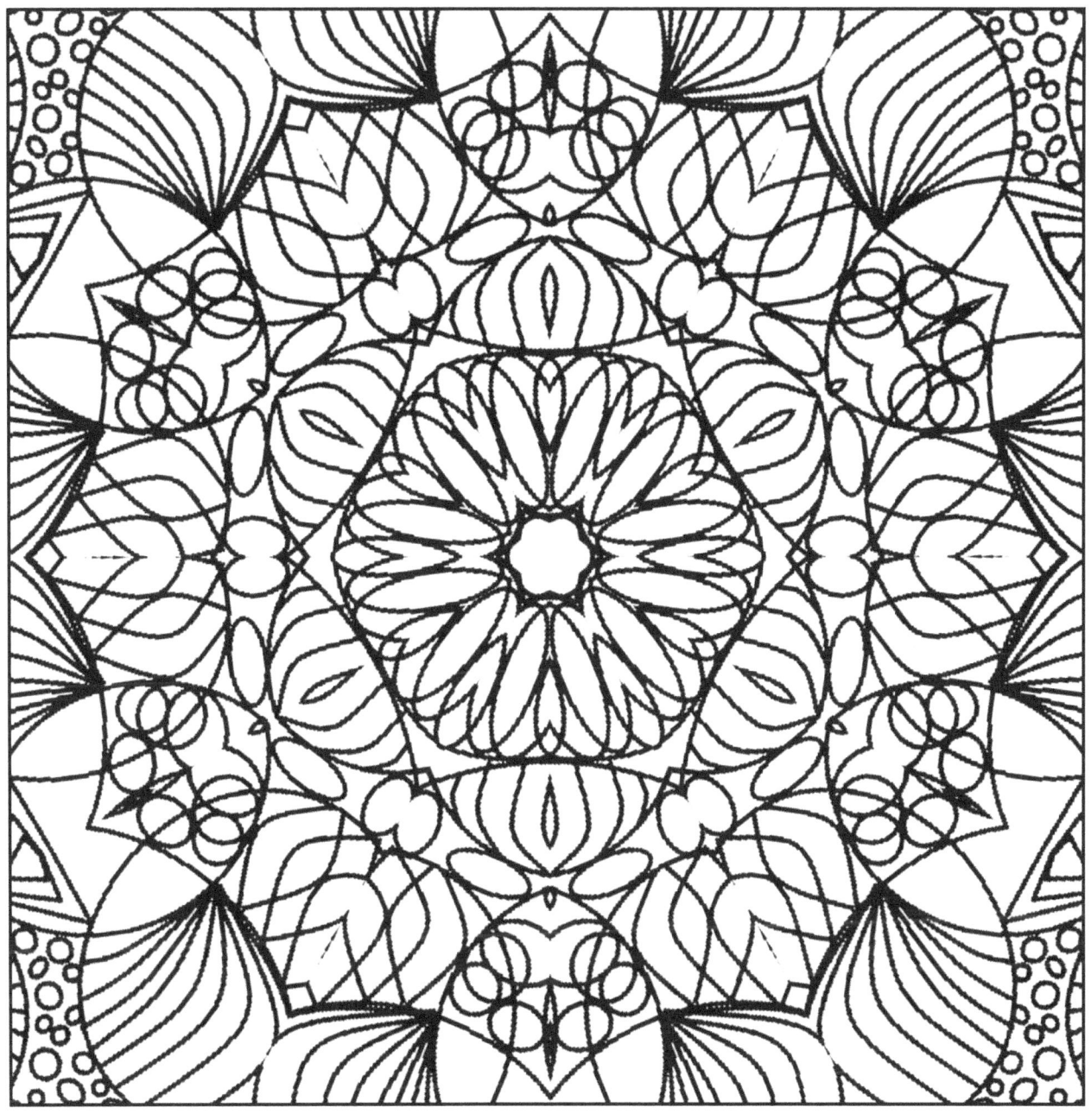

Happy Thought:

"If depression has taught me one thing, it is this: what a rare and beautiful treasure is the simple human gift of joy. For me now, joy - our capacity to delight in one another and in the world - is the reason why we are here. It is as simple as that. And I feel compelled to spread the word."

~~Giles Andreae~~

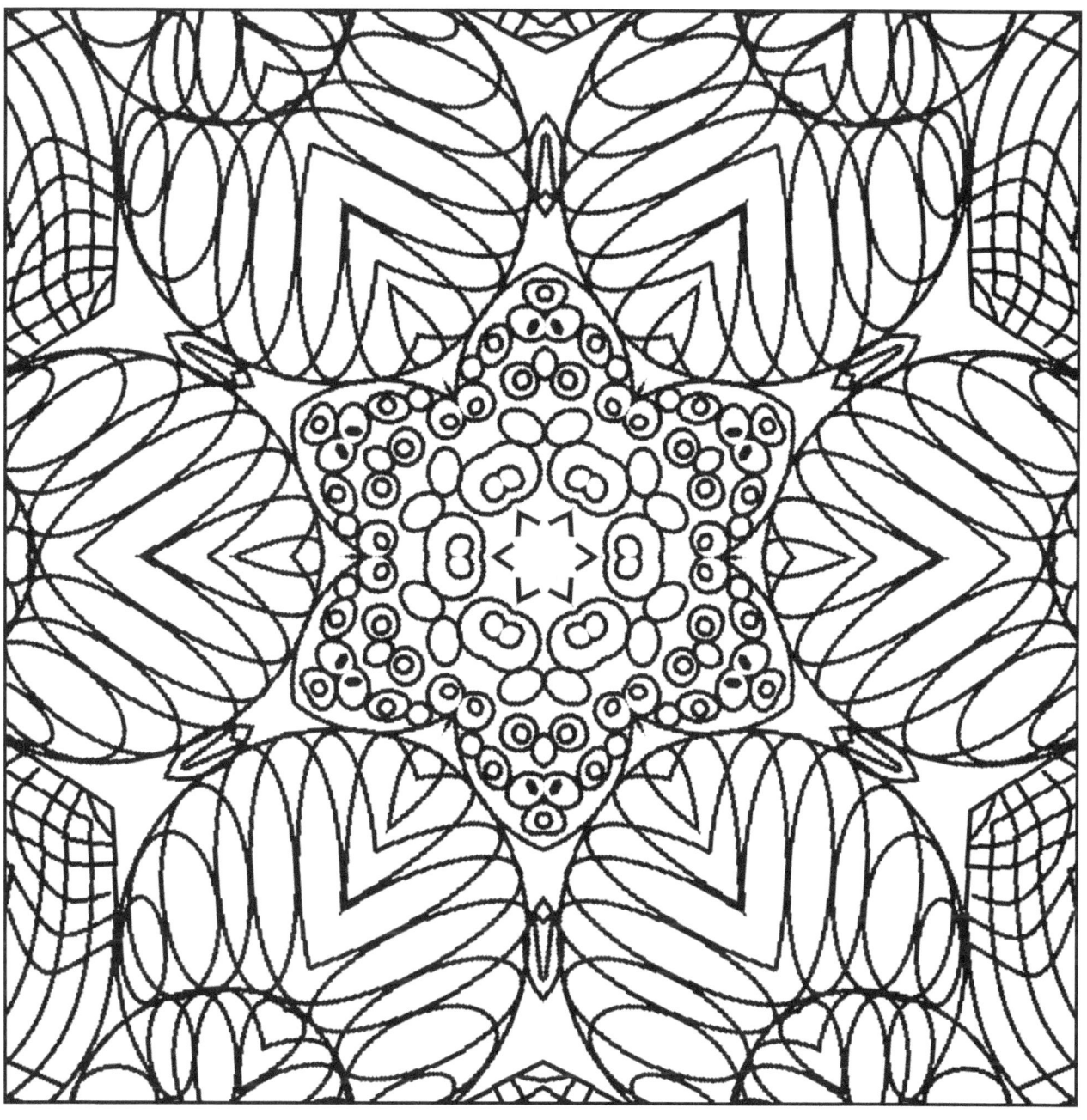

Happy Thought:

"The discipline of gratitude is the explicit effort to acknowledge that all I am and have is given to me as a gift of love, a gift to be celebrated with joy."

~~Henri Nouwen~~

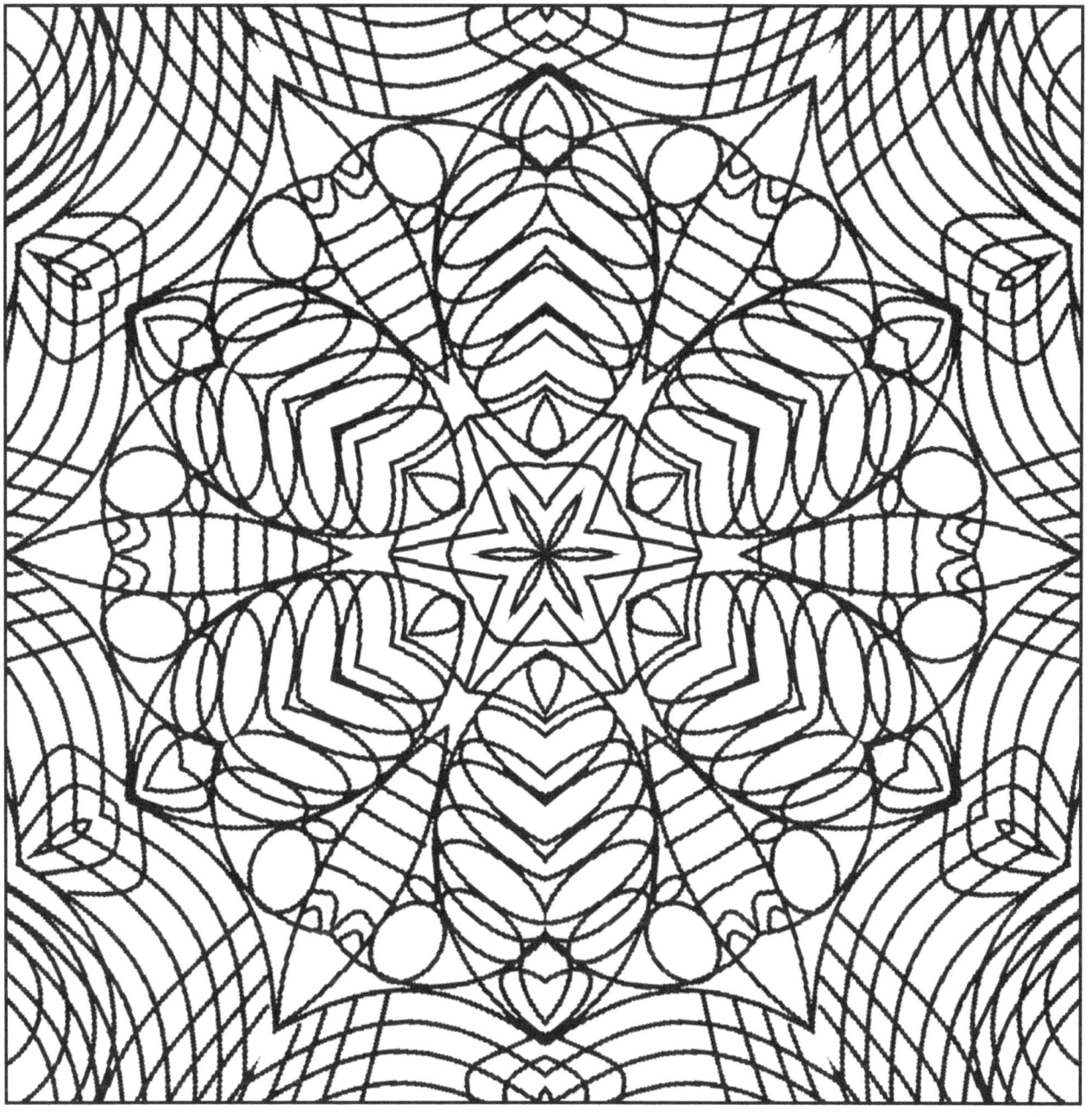

Happy Thought:

"When one is giving service for the advancement of humanity, when one is working without money and without price, with no hope of earthly reward, there comes a real, genuine joy into the human heart."

~~Heber J. Grant~~

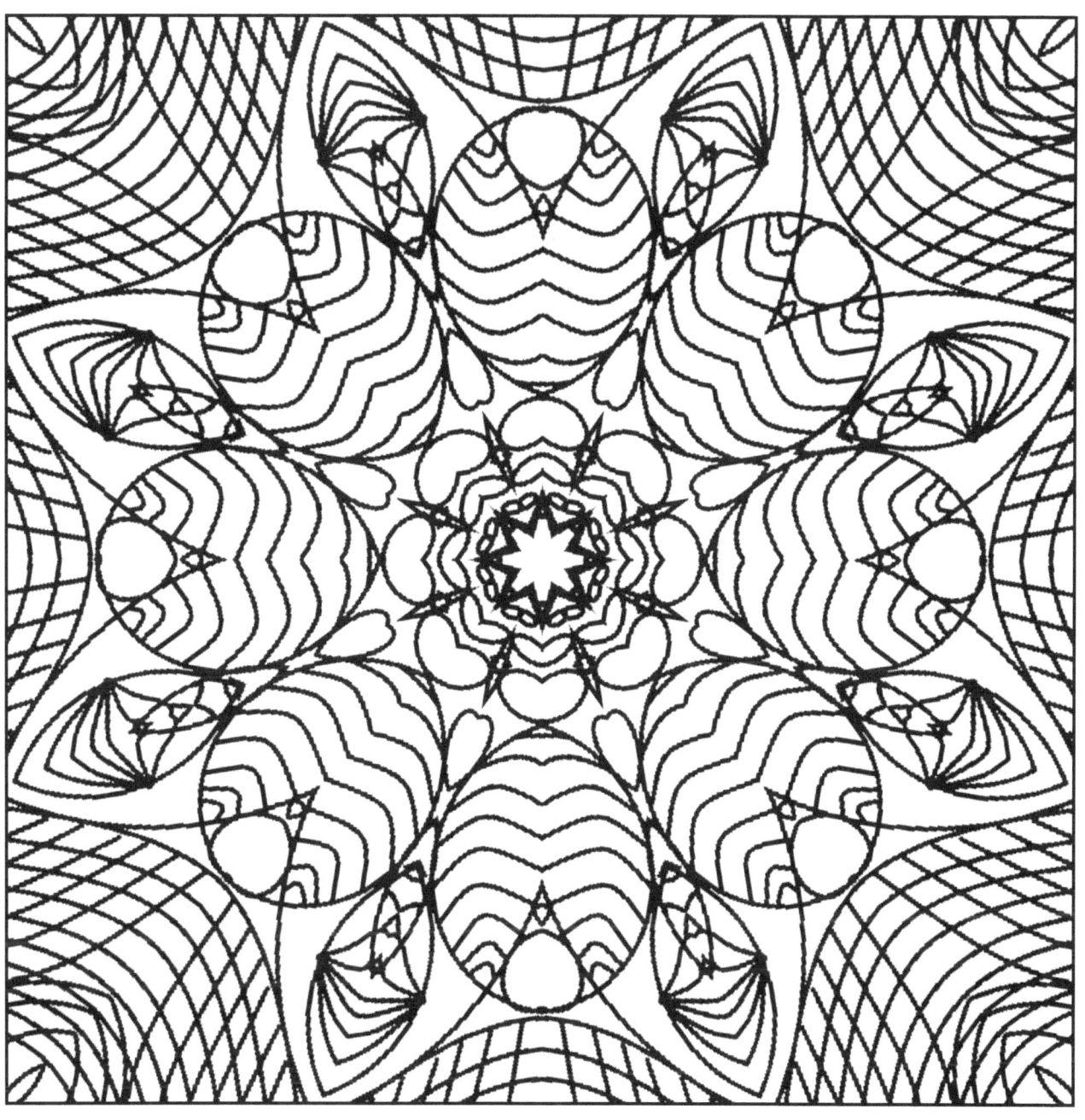

Happy Thought:

"Let a joy keep you. Reach out your hands and take it when it runs by."

~~Carl Sandburg~~

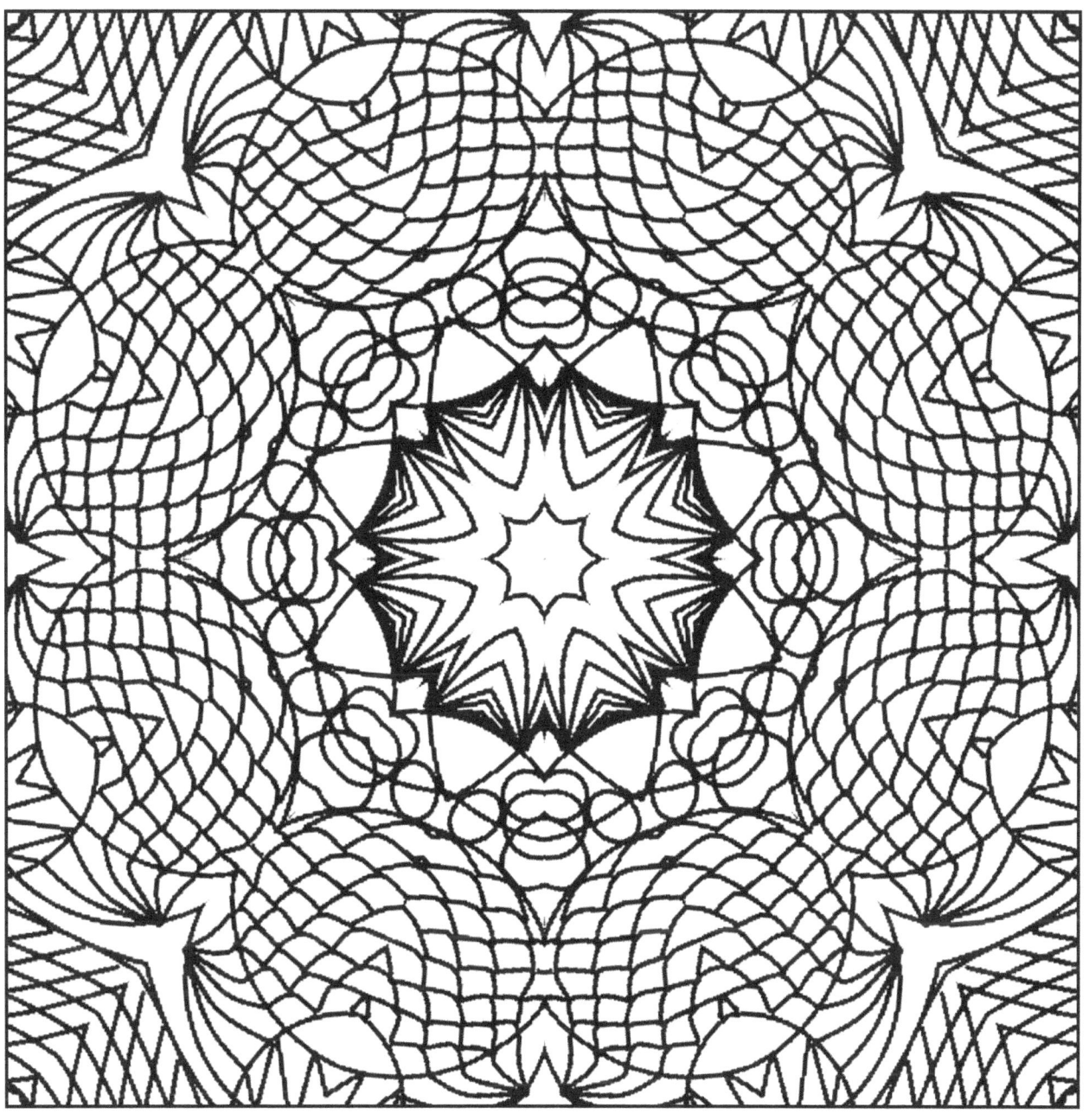

Happy Thought:

"You don't have to be Picasso or Rembrandt to create something. The fun of it, the joy of creating, is way high above anything else to do with the art form."

~~Chick Corea~~

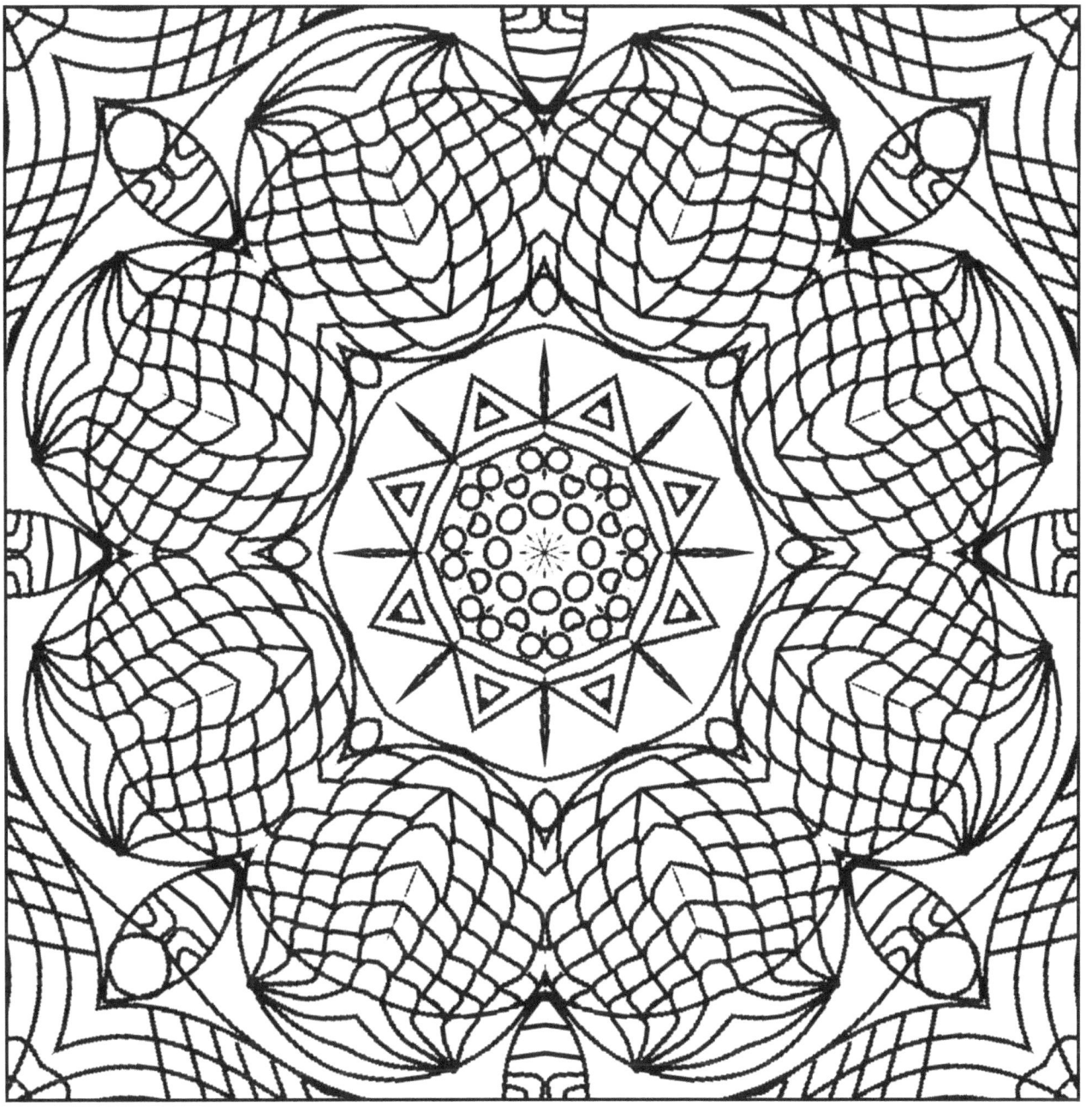

Happy Thought:

"Love is the fire that warms our lives with unparalleled joy and divine hope. Love should be our walk and our talk."

~~Dieter F. Uchtdorf~~